CW01085059

Finding Fame

Failure

Ambition

Mindset

Exercise

by

Paul Baker

**Grosvenor House
Publishing Limited**

All rights reserved
Copyright © Paul Baker, 2021

The right of Paul Baker to be identified as the author of this
work has been asserted in accordance with Section 78
of the Copyright, Designs and Patents Act 1988

The book cover is copyright to Paul Baker

This book is published by
Grosvenor House Publishing Ltd
Link House
140 The Broadway, Tolworth, Surrey, KT6 7HT.
www.grosvenorhousepublishing.co.uk

This book is sold subject to the conditions that it shall not, by way of
trade or otherwise, be lent, resold, hired out or otherwise circulated
without the author's or publisher's prior consent in any form of binding or
cover other than that in which it is published and
without a similar condition including this condition being imposed
on the subsequent purchaser.

A CIP record for this book
is available from the British Library

ISBN 978-1-83975-663-4

Contents

Introduction   ix

A Good Year   1

Line in the Sand   5

I Don't Like Mondays   13

Ultimate Truth   23

Baptism of Fire   33

Soldiering On   45

Failure not an Option   55

Smashing It   61

Almost There   69

Two Tribes   81

Shit, We're Going to Roll   89

Desire the Right   97

Stims to Holdfast   107

Ascension 1815   115

Realising the Dream   119

A Room with a View   129

Back to Life, Back to Reality   135

Poacher Turned Gamekeeper   143

Summit Fever   159

Giving Back   169

Kids, Sport & Holidays   183

Big Five Zero   191

Stay at Home   199

Does he fight it?   205

Epilogue   213

About the Author   217

Acknowledgements

Having an idea and turning it into a memoir has been both challenging and rewarding.

I want to thank my mum and dad, who taught me discipline and respect, and for giving me the confidence to succeed.

My sister and brother, for always having my back.

Jayne for always being there, and Andrew and Luke for making our family complete.

And, last but not least, I want to thank the middle school teacher for defining the line in the sand, Hanshi Steve Arneil for his karate teachings, and the boys who arrived at Bath railway station on the 4th January 1983.

Foreword

"Jessica Grace Coleman, personal development author"

Paul Baker has experienced many ups and downs in his life, but it's how he dealt with these moments and learned from them that really sets his story apart.

Covering themes such as ambition, failure, and the importance of mindset and exercise when it comes to personal growth, this book illustrates Paul's determination and drive to constantly improve both himself and his life.

Paul has enjoyed many major milestones over the years, from being awarded the Kyokushinkai Karate black belt at just age 16 to serving in the British Army, a career that led him all over the world to places like Belize and the Falkland Islands.

This book showcases how important it is to fail in life – to get knocked down but then to rise up again, stronger and wiser and ready for the next obstacle. His martial arts background and army training taught Paul the importance of discipline and resilience, traits he took with him and used in all other areas of his life. Underlining everything he does is his knowledge of how your mindset can set you up for success, and the understanding that bad experiences aren't ultimately bad, as they can teach you the tools and techniques you need to navigate through the challenges of life.

Paul also understands the power of setting goals in life, and in being ambitious with those goals. Without a clear, set plan, you won't know which direction to set off in – which path to take – and, even if you end up going down a path you hadn't previously considered, you simply have to take that first step. What you learn along the way is often far more important than the destination you initially had in mind.

Paul acknowledges the impact his environment had on him when he was younger, from his home life to his schooldays and his extracurricular activities. He attributes his positive growth mindset to several people from his youth: his parents, his middle school teacher, and his martial arts instructors. These individuals moulded who he was as a person and encouraged him to view circumstances and obstacles from a different perspective; by shifting his mindset, he opened himself up to all the wonderful opportunities this world has to offer.

Exercise is another key theme in the book; Paul looks at how it helped him both physically and mentally as he grew up. As he says, the earlier you start physical activity, the faster the payback – in all areas of your life. Not only does exercise improve your health and help with weight loss, but it also encourages a happier, more positive mindset, increases your energy levels, and gives you the confidence required to go after what you really want. Without exercise, Paul simply would not have accomplished everything he's achieved in his life so far.

This book is an excellent example of how mindset is everything, how failure is a learning experience, and that – in order to keep growing as a person – you simply must carry on, no matter what life throws at you.

Introduction

I was born in the summer of '66 – 21 years after the end of the Second World War – in one of the new towns built to assist with the overspill from London. I arrived the day after England had only managed a 0-0 result against Uruguay in their opening match of the World Cup tournament.

Just 18 days later, England went on to win their first ever FIFA World Cup at Wembley Stadium in front of the home nation. Manager Alf Ramsey had masterminded the nation's greatest ever sporting triumph.

Alf Ramsey found fame on a global stage through employing key traits that brought him the success he so desired.

Failure

The state or condition of not meeting a desirable or intended objective.

Ramsey had certainly witnessed failure: a 5-2 loss to France in a European Nations Cup qualifier, leading to the press questioning his appointment. In response to the failure, he took a major gamble by changing the formation of the team.

Ambition

A strong desire to do or achieve something typically requiring determination and hard work.

"We will win the World Cup," Ramsey announced with uncharacteristic bravado as he took over the national team reins in 1963.

Mindset

A set of assumptions, methods, or notations held by one or more people.

Ramsey possessed an astute football brain. He was a strict disciplinarian and technician well ahead of his time, and his greatest talent was utilising mindset to get the best out of his players.

Exercise

Activity requiring physical effort, carried out to sustain or improve health and fitness.

The winning squad of 1966 were credited as being the fittest in the tournament. In fact, Ramsey referred to it as 'England's USP' and was quoted in victory as saying, "We were the fastest and strongest side in the World Cup."

1

A GOOD YEAR

A Geoff Hurst hat-trick helped England lift the Jules Rimet trophy, the team beating West Germany 4-2 in extra time. Alf Ramsey had dispensed with the wingers mid-tournament, and had selected Geoff Hurst ahead of Jimmy Greaves in the final. Clearly, Ramsey's leadership made all the difference.

The final goal inspired one of the most famous commentary lines of all time from BBC's Kenneth Wolstenholme: *"Some people are on the pitch, they think it's all over... it is now."*

This time period – often referred to as the 'swinging sixties' – is considered by some as being the defining decade that brought about huge change for all those who lived through those times. This generation were starting to forget about the pain and hardship the Second World War had delivered, and London was starting to transform into the capital of the world: full of optimism, freedom, and promise.

This generation were the first free from conscription, and they were also finally given a voice and the freedom to do what they wanted. The parents of the sixties' teenage generation had spent their youths serving King and Country, and they desperately wanted their own children to have the freedoms the war had denied them.

Music dominated the period. Although rock and roll had dominated the 1950s, with groups like Bill Haley and the Comets, now it was time for British music to emerge, with The Beatles – a band from Liverpool – bursting onto the scene.

They continued the rock and roll genre for the early part of the sixties, but by 1967 they had released *Sgt. Pepper's Lonely Hearts Club Band*, which would become the turning point for popular music. The lyrics also started encouraging revolution against authorities, leading to the younger generation wanting to take a stand for their beliefs.

Mary Quant become famous for making the mini skirt popular; this became the height of 1960s fashion and allowed women to feel liberated and free. By the late sixties, vibrant colours started appearing on clothes as the hippie movement gathered momentum.

In 1961, President John F. Kennedy (JFK) gave his 'Moon Speech' to Congress, announcing his ambition to put a man on the moon by the end of the decade. He was also at the helm during the Cuban Missile Crisis, which brought the world very close to nuclear war.

In 1963 JFK was assassinated in Dallas, Texas whilst travelling in the presidential limousine en route to a political rally. He was taken to Parkland Hospital, where he was pronounced dead 30 minutes later. The assassination shocked the world and led to Lyndon B. Johnson being sworn in as President on the same day JFK was killed.

Meanwhile, the Profumo Affair was rocking the British establishment. It was a scandalous mix of sex, spies, and government, which took place during the height of the Cold War. The Secretary of State for War, John Profumo, was discovered to be having an affair with model and showgirl Christine Keeler, who was also involved with Soviet naval attaché, Yevgeny Ivanov. Profumo initially denied the affair but later admitted that he'd lied to the House of Commons, consequently resigning. The affair seriously undermined the public's trust in politicians, leading to suspicion between the people and the government.

At 9.32 a.m. on July 16th, 1969 – with the whole world watching – Apollo 11 took off from Kennedy Space Centre with astronauts Neil Armstrong, Buzz Aldrin, and Michael Collins on board. After travelling 240,000 miles, Apollo 11 entered the lunar orbit on July 19th, and the next day, Armstrong and Aldrin manned the Eagle Lunar Module, separated from the command module, and began descending to the lunar surface.

When the craft landed on the Sea of Tranquillity on the moon's surface at 4.17 p.m., Armstrong radioed Mission Control in Texas with his famous message, "The Eagle has landed".

At 10.56 p.m., as Armstrong stepped off the ladder and onto the moon's surface, he said his famous words: "That's one small step for man, one giant leap for mankind", cementing JFK's desire to send a man to the moon.

The sixties had started out bleak, but by the end of the decade people were full of hope and optimism as the seventies approached.

2

LINE IN THE SAND

In 1971 we moved into a brand new house on a cul-de-sac street in one of the newly constructed neighbourhoods within the town. These new neighbourhoods had been well designed, with each one being served by a school, a shopping parade, and community facilities, with open spaces aplenty. The town itself had been designed as several different neighbourhoods operating as independent hubs around a vibrant town centre, including a library and sport centre. A fast-growing industrial estate and Gatwick Airport were also situated within the town's boundary. This was a private development full of families who had been encouraged to leave congested London in order to support the growth of the new towns. Looking back, it must have seemed like a utopia for the generation leaving London. The town was well provided for, full of parks and open spaces, and it had easy access to both the countryside and coast.

I had a great childhood there, spending lots of time playing sports in the local park, riding my racing bike, annoying the neighbours, playing 'knock down ginger', and retrieving balls from back gardens. My earliest memories of school are really just vague recollections of playing marbles in the playground and football on the school field. It was apparent – due to the array of football shirts on display during PE lessons – that the majority of my school year had moved down from London, with Chelsea, Tottenham Hotspur, and Crystal Palace being the most popular.

I was the middle child, my sister having been born in 1963 and then my brother arriving in December 1972. My dad (who came from Brixton) and my mum (from Saint Mary Cray, Kent) had met at work, both of them believing that fate brought the two of them together. My dad had just returned from completing National Service, and one day he'd met up with his own father for a few drinks. As he left the pub, a car suddenly pulled up, the window was wound down, and a voice said:

"Is that you, Bill?"

"Yes," my dad replied.

"What are you doing out?"

"Seeing my dad; I've left the Army."

"Do you fancy your old job back?"

"Of course," my dad replied.

"Be at Brixton Town Hall at eight Monday morning. I'll pick you up."

And with that, the car was gone.

The following Monday, my dad waited at the town hall to meet his boss, and when he arrived at his place of work, he was met by his boss's secretary – my mum. He could have been in any pub at any time, but he just so happened to be leaving that one at exactly the same time his old boss was driving past. Thirty seconds either way, and their paths wouldn't have crossed.

My mum and dad dated for 18 months before getting married in 1961, when they moved into a one-bedroom flat together in Dulwich. The flat had a shared kitchen, an outside toilet, a small living area, and one bedroom. Times were hard, but they were both war children who'd been evacuated, so they were resilient and accustomed to hardship. After the birth of my sister, they decided to follow my grandparents down to the new town in search of a better life.

My early years at primary school flew by. I enjoyed most subjects apart from French – which I loathed with a passion – but I preferred sporting subjects over academic lessons, especially athletics and the gymnastic PE lessons. I also made lots of friends who all lived close to me, allowing me an exciting childhood with total freedom to roam, even at such a young age.

School was very different back then, and I was probably part of the last generation that were still taught using Victorian principles. The school was totally white, obesity was nowhere to be seen, and the 'school run' simply didn't exist as everybody walked. Mobile phones, social media etc. were years off in the future, so we had to make do with the art of conversation. Discipline and respect were rife, with misbehaviour being dealt with swiftly. This would come to the fore following the arrival of a new teacher from the north of England. I was wayward both at home and at school, so although I didn't know it at the time, I was about to be on a collision course with this new teacher.

My parents were old school – both of them strict – so discipline and respect were common threads throughout my entire childhood. Despite this approach, however, I was still a wayward child, though I (fortunately) kept myself in check as far as possible, with most of my discretions being merely mischievous rather than criminal. I was taught the importance of respect, the difference between right and wrong, and how to stand up for myself. My interest in Bruce Lee led to me taking up Judo at the age of nine, and Karate two years later. I carried on with gymnastics at school, I started running, and I began throwing myself into Judo, training at two clubs. I also started to get interested in the military; this was influenced by my dad, who spent a lot of time telling me all about his national service, especially his time in Northern Ireland and Cyprus. My interest grew even further when he decided to join the Territorial Army, taking him back on overseas tours – something I wanted to do as well.

The transition to middle school was made easy as both schools were joined, and nothing really changed apart from one key individual: the new teacher. My classmates remained the same, but now we had a thickset man standing in front of our class. He was solid, with a rugby prop body type, and therefore demanded a level of respect no one had ever seen before. There was no way anyone would cross him, not at the outset anyway. A few weeks later, I found out the consequences of upsetting him the hard way.

I was sitting in class, having just completed registration, when my mate slapped me around the back of the head out of the teacher's line of sight. I responded by striking back, this time under the teacher's full gaze, resulting in him walking over to me and extending his arm towards my head. He then grabbed the little hair I had on my head between his forefingers and thumb, twisting it around until my head was stuck firmly in his grip. I was pulled to my feet and forced to follow him swiftly out of the classroom. He stood over me and read me the riot act, warning me that I was lucky not to be sent to the headmaster. His body language told me he meant business; he didn't have to say anything else. This particular move was etched into school history, being coined 'the thumb grip'.

This practice was really effective as, most of the time, it had the desired effect of sorting out the wayward children; you learnt very quickly how to behave in his lessons. This practice wouldn't be allowed today, but I still believe these methods worked back then, as children were brought up with discipline and respect. I was wayward, but I still respected adults and authority, something that appears to be missing in today's society due to political correctness and the removal of policies and practices over time.

My teacher went on to become a highly regarded headmaster, and when I last saw him I thanked him for my education and for installing discipline and respect into my mindset. I also reminded him of his famous grip, which he didn't acknowledge or deny, simply stating, "They were different times back then."

I have many happy childhood memories that stick in my mind, including watching *Jaws* at the cinema and attending street parties celebrating the Queen's Silver Jubilee. *Jaws*, which was released in 1975, told the story of repeated shark attacks at holiday resort Amity Island. The film opens with a young woman being killed whilst skinny-dipping at night, her body parts being washed up on the shoreline the following morning. The local Police Chief, Brody, makes it his mission to destroy the killer shark, and there are lots of twists and turns along the way. At the time the film was really frightening, with many scenes making the whole audience jump. The film's score was notable too. Consisting of an alternating pattern of just two notes, the main theme delivered suspense and danger – which increased in tone as the shark edged ever nearer to the victim.

This film changed everything that was linked to swimming. No one wanted to get back into the sea for fear of a shark attack, and it even meant I was checking for sharks before diving into swimming pools. The film was life changing for me, with the iconic theme music entering my head every time I entered water.

The Silver Jubilee was another significant event, marking the 25th anniversary of the Queen's accession to the thrones of the United Kingdom and Commonwealth realms. Throughout the whole year there were enormous street parties and events taking place across the country, with our street party taking place in June of that year. Our party was a mass of red, white, and blue bunting, with Union Jack flags being plastered everywhere. Tables and chairs lined the road to create a large eating area, where all the families sat around to enjoy burgers and sausages cooked by the dads. The party continued long into the night, with lots of activities and music being played and with all the children receiving the Queen Elizabeth silver commemorative coin.

During the same year, I also recall the Sex Pistols releasing their own version of the national anthem, which of course was perceived as being totally anti-establishment and anti-royalist. I would get to experience the whole punk crusade a year later at secondary school.

I continued practising Judo three times a week, allowing a quick progression through the belts, and I also joined the Royal Marines Cadets to seek insight into the military, so my spare time was well utilised. I took to the Cadets straight away, enjoying the military syllabus and taking pride in wearing the uniform. I recall being taught about the history of the Corps, as well as the motto, which is still stuck firmly in my mind: 'Per Mare, Per Terram', or 'By Sea, By Land'. Even though I didn't usually enjoy academic subjects, I took to this learning really easily, making me realise that if I actually was interested in a subject, I would want to learn.

The Cadets allowed me to enjoy many exciting activities including field craft, weapon handling, and map reading – all essential skills that would benefit me during my basic training five years later. It also meant that we got to carry out activities on water, such as sailing and powerboating around Portsmouth Harbour under the gaze of HMS Ark Royal. I remained in the Cadets for over four years, reluctantly having to leave so I could concentrate solely on Karate. Even so, I gained valuable experience during my time in the Cadets that I would draw upon later in my career.

I took to all forms of exercise, enjoying all sport but choosing running and martial arts as my main interests. Exercise became part of my daily routine, with walking to school, PE lessons, and participating in sports after school all becoming part of my DNA. Respect and discipline had been implanted into my mindset from both my parents and the teachers at school, and so I knew these were important skills to harvest, both of them becoming values I would go on to adopt myself. I was still a pretty wayward kid, but I managed to strike a balance between what was deemed acceptable behaviour and what was not. The two should not go together, but in my case they did. I also had ambition: to do well and to achieve the personal goals I set for myself.

My early childhood had prepared me well for the transition to secondary school. I'd heard a lot of bullying happened there, but having experienced bullying first-hand I wasn't too worried about the rumours that were circulating. With middle school over, it was time to prepare for secondary school; the next big chapter of my life was coming fast.

3

I DON'T LIKE MONDAYS

For students waiting to start secondary school, there were lots of rumours around – particularly regarding bullying, dress code, and discipline. Bullying was a regular talking point towards the end of middle school, and dress code was an unknown as the school had no uniform policy. This was the place where children from different neighbourhoods across town would come together, face to face, for the first time. This was important, as the pecking order had already been established throughout middle school at the neighbourhood level, but now it was back to square one and so it would have to be re-established. In September 1978, at the age of twelve, I attended my first day at secondary school, long before Facebook, Instagram, Snapchat and Twitter were on the scene. Instead the subcultures of the school were punk, skinhead and mod.

Dressed in blue jeans, Dr. Martens boots, and a red Harrington jacket (and with a number 2 crew cut) I walked into the school playground trying desperately not to bring any unwanted attention to myself. I was immediately drawn to two boys standing in the corner of the tennis courts, the first a skinhead dressed similarly to myself. He stood talking to a Pakistani boy – an unusual sight for me, this being the first time I'd seen a person of colour at school. I later found out that the skinhead was his best mate, who'd managed to establish himself at the top of the pecking order at middle school and no doubt would want to gain his title again at this new, next level.

The first term was spent making new friends, meeting teachers, learning the timetable, and coming to terms with the homework overload. Physical Education (PE) quickly became my favourite subject, unlike the other academic lessons that I didn't really enjoy. My PE teacher was Welsh, so during the winter months we played his favourite sport, rugby – in all weathers. When not playing rugby we would all have to compete in the mob run, a three-mile woodland course around the adjacent park and forest. I loved this race and I was good at it too, always finishing in the top three and earning respect from the PE staff.

School assemblies would include government information videos, which would mostly warn us that no part of the United Kingdom was safe due to the imminent threat of nuclear war. It was widely reported that due to its close proximity to Gatwick Airport, our home town was considered a strategic target and would therefore be one of the first areas likely to be hit. With the election of Margaret Thatcher in 1979, and Ronald Reagan in the US in 1980, there had been a corresponding change in western policy towards the Soviet Union. The threat of nuclear war had reached new heights not seen since the Cuban Missile Crisis.

We learnt about the effects of nuclear fallout, planning for survival, and how to recognise the warning signs when an attack was imminent. We also learnt what to do immediately after the attack, as well as in the days thereafter. I remember being told that if you were caught outside in the open during a nuclear strike, you should fall to the floor as quickly as possible, lay flat, and cover up any exposed skin. You were also instructed to look away from ground zero, the point on the ground directly under the nuclear detonation.

I had taken history and was learning about the Second World War, from the invasion of Poland –resulting in Britain declaring war on Germany – to the end of war, when American President Franklin D. Roosevelt ordered the bombing of Hiroshima and Nagasaki. The atomic bomb dropped on Hiroshima devastated an area of five square miles, destroying over 60% of the city and killing 140,000 people. I was living four miles from Gatwick, in a town with a population of around 80,000, and after doing the maths, we quickly came to the conclusion that any advice given during assemblies would be rendered useless.

Exercise and sport continued to play significant roles in my life. Judo and karate were at the forefront of my hobbies, and I worked hard to attain the higher grades. I was also very much into running, the reason I excelled in the mob run. For this I had two local role models: Daley Thompson, who I'd see training down at the local athletics track, and the boxer Alan Minter, who I often saw out and about going through his training routine.

Daley Thompson won Gold in all four major competitions: the Olympics, the World Championships, the Commonwealth Games, and the European Championships. Alan Minter won Bronze at the 1972 Olympics, and after defeating Vito Antuofermo at Caesars Palace, he became Middleweight Champion of the World in 1980. I was lucky enough to witness these two people first-hand as they reached the top of their respective sports, and I felt incredibly proud that they were both linked to my home town.

I was popular at school, but my constant waywardness meant I was always getting in trouble with my teachers, something that resulted in me spending lots of time in detention, though I was too smart to receive the cane or slipper. I would mess about all the time, seeing how far I could push the teachers, but I always seemed to know when to stop, or – if needed – disappear off the radar completely. My theory was proven during a school strike, when many students refused to enter the school gates for no apparent reason. We sat outside in a large group and sang out the lyrics to 'We Don't Need No Education'.

The protest went on all morning, before it was brought to a swift end when the headmaster finally decided to come out and join the party. Despite many pupils being suspended for participating in the strike, I managed to come away unmarked, though I wasn't sure why. Perhaps it was because I managed to disappear just before the strike ended; thankfully, this was years before CCTV and mobile phone footage would have put me at the scene.

Bullying was part of normal school life, but I was never on the receiving end of it. When you were at school it was the law of the jungle, so you had to stand up for yourself or run the risk of becoming a victim. I learnt that fast, just as I learnt that conflict mostly came from the many different subgenres in the school. In my school year it was the mods to be weary of – in particular, one boy who'd earnt the reputation of being the hardest boy in our year group. One day I was sitting in tutor group when a good friend of mine made a passing comment, stating that, "He wasn't scared of the mod." In today's world, this would be posted on Facebook or Instagram in seconds and the mod would have known immediately, but back then it took until lunchtime for the news to reach him. Unfortunately for my friend, during that time the story had become exaggerated to him wanting to 'take the mod out'. This resulted in the mod tracking him down in his lunch period, and – without warning – punching him hard in the face and splitting his mouth wide open. Case closed, no debate, a hard lesson to learn: "Be careful what you say, and who you say it to."

Music defined my school years, with fashion being dictated by the many different genres of music out there. I was a skinhead, influenced heavily by Ian Dury and the Blockheads, and the album *New Boots and Panties!!* was a must-have playlist for boys going through puberty. The songs covered a wide range of musical types including funk, disco, and rock and roll. These songs appealed to me as they were character-based stories containing lots of profanity, affection, and humour within the lyrics. My favourite tracks were *Sweet Gene Vincent*, *Wake Up And Make Love With Me*, and *Billericay Dickie*.

The other song that caught my attention was *I Don't Like Mondays* by the Boomtown Rats, which was written about the 1979 Cleveland Elementary School shooting in San Diego, California, where 16-year-old Brenda Ann Spencer went on a shooting spree in a school playground, killing two adults and injuring one police officer and eight school children. When interviewed by the police, Spencer gave no reason for her crimes other than her famous quote, "I don't like Mondays, this livens up the day." Bob Geldof was in Atlanta when the news broke and her reasoning led to the lyrics of the famous song.

The no uniform policy at school meant that you could dress according to whichever subculture you belonged at the time, with a wide range of fashions and musical influences to choose from. This was the early eighties, after all, and music had exploded. There were punk rockers walking around in tight tartan trousers with 'God Save The Queen' t-shirts, mods dressed in long green parkas over Fred Perry t- shirts, and skinheads in green bomber jackets, tight bleached jeans, and tanned Dr. Martens boots. I soon moved away from the full skinhead look, choosing a new fashion recognised as two tone now that Madness, The Specials, and The Selecter were my new musical influences.

Influenced by David Bowie and Roxy Music, a new group started to appear at school that I would soon discover was called the new romantics, as bands like Duran Duran, Spandau Ballet, and Ultravox burst onto the music scene; these all pushed the fashion envelope even further for makeup, hairstyles, and clothing.

Girls also entered my world around this time, as we'd hang out together at school discos. My limited knowledge of girls and no sexual experience, however, meant I was on the back foot. Boys in my year were considered far too immature and were therefore mostly ignored by the girls, who would only date the older boys. Consequently we were left with a small number of girls to choose from, meaning competition was fierce. I didn't do too badly, however; I actually ended up going out with one of the popular girls in that school year, though it didn't last long before she got rid of me, for lack of sexual experience on my part. If I wanted girls to hang around for more than four weeks, I knew I'd have to up my game in that area.

It was now 1982, and I was in the last six months of my education. My constant waywardness gave me little hope of staying on for A levels, and besides, I had no appetite for university. My ambitions for the year were to pass army selection and earn the right to wear a black belt in karate, though putting so much effort into karate training meant I had to drop judo. I'd also commenced the selection process for the army, and was busy training hard in preparation for my upcoming grading. As well as this, I had to prepare for summer exams as I needed a good set of results to satisfy the army board. This period of time, therefore, proved intensely busy, with little time for anything else.

By 1982, unemployment had exceeded 3,000,000 – a new post-war record. These were worrying times, particularly if you were leaving school that year; the general perception was that you'd be leaving school just to join a very long dole queue. The country was losing patience with the government due to domestic policies, deep spending cuts, and the high unemployment rates.

Then, during April of that year, events suddenly took a dramatic turn. I remember being told at school that the Malvinas had been invaded by Argentina. No one had ever heard of this place before, and more importantly, no one knew it was a British dependant territory. It soon became apparent that the United Kingdom was preparing to go to war with Argentina over a little known set of islands located in the South Atlantic: the Falklands.

Margaret Thatcher had set a precedent two years earlier when the Iranian Embassy, located at Prince's Gate in London, was stormed by six terrorists from the KSA group, who were campaigning for Arab national sovereignty in the southern region of Khuzestan Province, Iran; they took over twenty people hostage, including embassy workers and visitors. It was clear that, during the early stages of the siege, police negotiations were failing. The situation was worsening day by day, and on the sixth day one of the hostages was killed and thrown out onto the street in front of the waiting media. With seemingly no end in sight, Margaret Thatcher gave orders for the Special Air Service (SAS) to storm the building and rescue the remaining hostages. This lasted just 17 minutes, with the SAS rescuing all but one of the hostages and killing five out of the six terrorists. That day, the iconic film footage of the SAS abseiling from the roof of the embassy was etched onto history forever, and this operation – known as Operation Nimrod – brought the SAS out of the shadows and into the spotlight for the very first time.

Margaret Thatcher had stood firm from day one of the siege, coordinating the actions of the government in response to the national crisis, and she went on to issue the following statement: "No terrorist will leave the UK under any circumstances. No hostage will leave the UK under pressure."

Living up to her nickname of 'the Iron Lady', Thatcher turned the statement into an official UK policy – a policy of no surrender. It was reported that she'd wanted the whole event to be shown live on television in the hope of sending out a tough message to the watching world.

On 2nd April 1982, Argentine forces carried out amphibious landings on the Falkland Islands, the troops overcoming the small defence party of Royal Marines based at Moody Brook Barracks to the west of Port Stanley. The following day the associated island of South Georgia was seized, and by late April there were ten thousand plus troops based on the island, the vast majority being conscripts.

Within three days Margaret Thatcher had ordered a naval task force of over 11,000 military personnel to travel 8,000 miles into the South Atlantic in order to recapture the islands. On April 5th, Thatcher told the ITN News, "We must recover the Falkland Islands for Britain and for the people who live there who are of British stock."

The British Government declared a war zone – which stretched 200 miles around the Falklands –and quickly assembled a naval force made up of HMS Hermes and HMS Invincible, as well as the two cruise ships, Queen Elizabeth 2 and the Canberra. Amazingly, within three days of the invasion the task force set sail from Portsmouth Harbour, and were later reinforced on route.

The British landed unopposed at the beachhead at San Carlos, as the Argentinians had expected the landings to take place at Port Stanley. It wasn't long, however, before the Argentine air forces started attacking the British fleet, resulting in the sinking of two frigates, one destroyer and one container ship. Under adverse weather conditions, the British forces advanced rapidly towards the capital, capturing the settlements of Darwin and Goose Green. After days of hard fighting – some of it hand-to-hand – against dug in troops along several ridgelines, the British succeeded in occupying the high ground around Port Stanley; they blockaded the capital and main port, cutting off the Argentine garrison. This led to Argentina's surrender on June 14th, 1982, ending the conflict. Argentina announced that 650 lives had been lost, whilst Britain's losses were 255.

The Iranian Embassy Siege was seen as one of Margaret Thatcher's greatest moments, and just two years later the invasion of the Falklands bolstered her reputation, her strong and decisive leadership giving the Conservative Party a decisive victory. The significant shift in public opinion seen after the victory in the Falklands essentially saved Margaret Thatcher and her government.

Watching the Iranian embassy siege and seeing the Falklands War unfold were major influences on my life, further cementing my desire to join the military. The SAS storming the embassy really was breathtaking, and I was in awe of all the secrecy surrounding the Special Forces. I had the utmost respect for all the military personnel who went to the Falklands; they'd left British summertime to fight a war 8,000 miles away during harsh winter conditions – with no time to prepare and on an island they knew nothing about – against an enemy who had over six weeks to prepare and establish themselves.

I enjoyed my time at secondary school; despite my constant waywardness I got through it unscathed and achieved the exam results required to qualify for army selection, although I would still need to pass the rigid selection process comprising both written and physical tests. I had started secondary school learning about the nuclear threat from the Soviet Union, and I finished my final year watching the events of the Falklands War unfold. Within three years of leaving school I would be playing out the Cold War for real in Germany, followed by tours to the British Military Hospital (BMH), the Falkland Islands, and the jungle of Central America, where I'd get to work with the SAS.

With my exams completed, it was now time to get my head down and concentrate on army selection, where events would lead me up to Scotland for two weeks of adventurous training. Many hours also needed to be spent at my dojo in preparation for my black belt grading.

4

ULTIMATE TRUTH

Whilst practising Judo at the recreation huts, I got to hear about a karate instructor who had trained in Japan and who was now teaching in the same neighbourhood as my judo club. I also found out that this person was credited with being the first non-Japanese national to complete the 100 man-Kumite, which entailed fighting 100 men one after another, for a duration of one and a half minutes per bout.

As my childhood hero was Bruce Lee, I grew up watching films like *Fist of Fury* and *Enter the Dragon*. I was excited, therefore, to hear about a karate master teaching nearby who sounded as iconic as my hero, and I decided to visit his club. The style of karate he taught was called Kyokushinkai – which I discovered translated to 'ultimate truth' – with the training being rooted in a philosophy of self-improvement, discipline, and hard work. I was hooked straightaway.

Initially, I attended these karate lessons twice a week. Discipline appeared to be at the heart of every session, with us having to enter and leave the dojo with a bow, as well as having to address all instructors by their grade. All sessions started with a show of respect to the Shihan, and would finish promptly with a period of reflection, undertaken in the kneeling position with our eyes closed. All students would then collectively thank Shihan and the instructors for teaching them.

I trained there for three months, learning all the techniques needed to gain my first belt. My parents bought me my Gi (suit), which featured the two badges that symbolised Kyokushinkai. There was some calligraphy worn high on the left side of the jacket, depicted in Japanese characters in a stylised form, and then the Kanku, which was placed above the left elbow. I learnt that Kyoku meant 'Ultimate', Shin 'Truth', and Kai 'Association'. The Kanku was derived from the Kanku Dai Kata, meaning 'Sky Gazing form'. I also learnt that the points of the Kanku represented fingers implying ultimate peaks, the wrists implying power, and the centre circle representing infinity, implying depth. It was clear that I had to quickly get to grips with the spiritual and philosophical components I'd now signed up to.

It also soon became evident that practising Kyokushinkai meant more than just being good at technique; personal fitness was also important, with an emphasis on stamina and strength. The spirituality and philosophy taught by the Shihan was tested at the first grading. I had to demonstrate the correct wearing of the Gi, the meaning of Kyokushinkai, and dojo etiquette, which included having to recite the dojo oath. I had to exhibit three basic stances, two types of punch, two blocks, and kicks. Punches had to be delivered to different body parts and performed whilst moving in different stances. I also had to demonstrate that I could speak and understand basic Japanese words, as well as counting up to ten.

We formed up in grade order to receive the result from Shihan, and I was informed that I had jumped one grade, being awarded the 9th Kyu white belt. I was really pleased, thinking I was now on my way. We were warned, however, that we had only just started the Kyokushinkai journey, that the training would get harder, and that he would expect the highest of standards at all times.

After twelve months of training, the Shihan opened up about his time in Japan and, more importantly, the 100-man Kumite. He told us he was born in South Africa and had immigrated to Northern Rhodesia as a child. Whilst living in Northern Rhodesia, he caught sight of a Chinese man practising martial arts in his garden, and – becoming totally mesmerised – he wanted to understand what the man was doing. One day, the man shouted out to Shihan and asked him if he wanted to study Shaolin Kempo, and he decided to start training straightaway. Shihan told me that he was always pulled to the Far East, so he decided to go travelling throughout South East Asia, including China, but only for a short period due to the political unrest in the country. He then decided to head back to Hong Kong to carry on with his training in Kempo. The training didn't really suit him, however, and whilst he was there he was told of a man called Mas Oyama, who was teaching karate in Japan.

In 1961 he arrived in Japan to commence training at Oyama's karate school, but when he arrived at the dojo, Mas Oyama wasn't there. Shihan was told to turn up at the dojo every day and wait for his arrival, and this went on for six weeks until he finally arrived. Shihan knew that this form of karate was very different from other styles, and was also very selective. When Mas Oyama finally arrived at the dojo, he went up to Shihan and told him, "Remember, you asked me to train you, I didn't ask you. You don't follow the rules, you're out. Understand?"

Shihan started training for six hours every day, and when he wasn't training he would have to clean and iron all of the instructor's Gis, as well as making the dojo spotless. The training was hard, with a mix of warm-ups, stretching, exercises such as push-ups/sit-ups, sparring, and Kata. It soon became apparent that the training methods taught to us by Shihan had been derived all those years earlier in Japan, and I could now fully understand why his training methods were so hard.

In 1965, Mas Oyama asked Shihan if he would like to attempt the 100-man Kumite, knowing that he would be the first non-Japanese person to be considered for this, and also knowing that all the other people who had tried this test had failed. He was told that he didn't have to win every fight, but that he just had to have the spirit to keep going and be prepared not to give up, regardless of what his opponents threw at him. He was also told that he would not know the date of the test. Shihan agreed, and Mas Oyama devised his training plan, ensuring he had the right fitness levels and attitude in order to complete the test.

He told me that on the day of the test he turned up for training as normal, but immediately sensed that there was a different atmosphere at the dojo. This was confirmed when Mas Oyama told him he would be fighting.

The test took two and three-quarter hours to complete. When he told me about this, he recalled that when a man named Tadashi Nakamura came out to fight him, he knew the top fighters were starting to appear, which signalled that he was coming to the end of the test. Ultimately he was successful, being recognised as only the second person in history to complete it. He didn't go into much detail about the bouts, but I remember him telling me that his body was battered and bruised by the end of it and that he collapsed in tears of pain when he saw his wife, who had to then walk him home. This achievement took place in 1965, and over half a century later there are less than thirty people worldwide who have successfully completed it. I felt privileged that he took the time to tell me how his interest in Shaolin Kempo, and his subsequent journey to Japan, had led him to take part in one of the most ultimate tests of body and mind. I was also struck by how modest he was, particularly the manner in which he told me the facts around his story.

He finished by telling me that in 1965, Mas Oyama asked him to leave Japan and travel to Britain, to spread the word about Kyokusinkai. He accepted, travelling to London to set up the first Kyokushin dojo in Stratford. It didn't take long before the style was earning a good reputation.

I was eleven years old by this time, training four hours a week, working through the syllabus, and advancing through the grades. I was promoted to 3rd Kyu, green belt, after two years of training. It was relentless, especially as during wintertime the dojo had no heating and at times no electricity, and we had to rely solely on

paraffin heating and lighting, making conditions harsh –
particularly during cold periods.

Standards of discipline were high; we were practising
Kyokushinkai, and that came with a cost, considering it was
recognised as the strongest form of karate. Shihan made sure that
the standards reflected the reputation of the style, always saying
that he "would prefer to teach five dedicated students than twenty
students who would turn up just to go through the motions."
Training got so tough that whenever I walked up to the dojo, my
heart would sink when I saw Shihan's car in the car park, and
I would breathe a sigh of relief when it wasn't. This was because I
knew I'd be in for two hours of physically demanding training
when he was at the dojo. I didn't appreciate this at the time, but
looking back, that training set me up for life.

A key part of the syllabus was Kata, which is executed as a
specified series of variety moves, stepping and turning whilst
maintaining perfect form, either undertaken on your own or as a
group. Kata was an integral part of the training, with many hours
spent perfecting moves, like a well-oiled army unit undertaking
drill at a ceremonial duty. Katas increased in difficulty, with new
techniques being introduced that forced us to learn how to use
different body parts to attack and defend.

At 3rd Kyu I had extensive knowledge about Kyokushinkai,
advanced techniques, and Kata, and being good at sparring and
having high fitness levels were pre-requisites. I had been training
for over three years by this point, working towards 2nd Kyu,
brown belt, and increasing my training to six hours per week.

As I turned up for grading I met a champion fighter, who watched
me as I went through my notes doing some last-minute revision.
After a while he turned to me and said, "If you don't know it by
now, you never will," and he had a point. I have always
remembered those poignant words, and as I'd been trained by
Shihan, I knew I was fully prepared. Those words would ring true

all the way through my career, with the motto 'Proper Planning and Practice Prevents Piss Poor Performance' becoming a management style that I would adopt time and time again.

I smashed the grading, winning the right to wear the brown belt and, following a similar training regime, twelve months later I was awarded 1st Kyu. I was now just one belt away from a Shodan, black belt (1 stripe), and earning the title Sempai.

One of my favourite memories of karate was taking part in the annual camp, which took place at Exeter University during the summer holidays. This was a week-long camp where the crème de la crème of the organisation would come together to teach masterclasses to eager students. You have to remember, these camps took place at the tail end of the seventies/early eighties, when life was very different, long before safeguarding and before children were wrapped up in cotton wool. The training would start long before sunrise, with a long run around the campus followed by syllabus training, finishing with sitting in the kneeling position in grade order. We were told to close our eyes for fifteen minutes for quiet reflection, and we would use this time as recovery and for quiet contemplation. This was always timed to coincide with the sun coming up, so you would close your eyes during darkness and open them in time to capture the full sunrise.

The day was split into morning and afternoon sessions, where the emphasis was on syllabus training, Kata, sparring, and fitness. There was also the infamous 'night run', where you'd be woken up in the very early hours, told to get into your Gi, and made to run between twenty to thirty minutes before going back to bed. This would happen at least twice, and the following morning you would still have to be up for training before breakfast.

I spent hours training at the dojo for my black belt, focusing on basic and advanced techniques, becoming proficient at performing techniques in Gyaku (techniques executed in reverse) as well as advanced Kata, and teaching the syllabus to other students.

Sparring had to be of the highest standard, and we had to be able to demonstrate a significant increase in stamina, as gradings were renowned for their gruelling fitness tests. I desperately wanted to achieve 1st Dan by sixteen – a great achievement, I thought. Kyokushinkai is well respected throughout the martial arts world, so there was a real prestige involved with being awarded a black belt, and even more so if the examiner was Shihan.

I arrived at the grading venue with the other candidates, who were all making nervous conversation about how we'd prepared and whether we were going to be good enough to pass. I did feel nervous, but also confident that I was going to be successful, considering I'd pushed myself through a rigorous training regime. The conversation seemed to be more about everyone fearing Shihan, as for most, summer camps were the only time their paths would ever cross. Personally, I'd gained an advantage by training under him for the past five years, but I was grounded enough to realise that he wouldn't be doing me any favours; if anything, I would need to be at the top of my game if I was going to be successful.

We lined up in single file, rank order with nowhere to hide. We then stood in Fudo-Dachi (basic stance) and bowed to Shihan, who told us, "You should be well prepared as you are going to be tested on all basic and advanced techniques. You will need to show me that you can teach, demonstrate a high level of fitness, and have full knowledge to meet the Shodan syllabus." We then introduced ourselves by name, grade, and resident dojo before commencing the grading.

After the warm-up we went through all techniques up to 5 Kyu, demonstrating Katas one after another in quick succession. We then had to teach three techniques to the other students, followed by performing two senior Katas, with Shihan watching our every move. Every time a student messed up their technique or got a question wrong, Shihan would make a point of turning to me or his other student to demonstrate the technique, or to answer the question, knowing we were both fully prepared. It soon become apparent who his students were.

We then undertook the fitness testing, comprising shuttle runs, 70 push-ups, 150 sit-ups, and 100 squats. Once completed, we had to demonstrate Tameshiwari (wood breaking), first with fist, then by elbow. The remainder of the grading was taken up with syllabus techniques through to Shodan, including the Tensho and Saiha (Katas) individually, with the other students watching and providing critique. Thirty minutes of Jiyu Kumite, covering three minute rounds, concluded the five-hour grading. We formed back up in Fudo-Dachi to be told the grading was over, and that the results would be published later that week.

Three days later I was informed that I had passed the grading and was awarded Shodan (1st Dan black belt), a great achievement at sixteen. There was real kudos with wearing your black belt around your Gi; it demanded a level of respect within the martial arts world that I wasn't accustomed to, and it was even more prevalent amongst karate students. I was praised by Shihan, who presented me with a temporary belt; my actual black belt – which had my name engraved into it – arrived from Tokyo a few weeks later. I found it fulfilling that I'd started karate five years earlier simply because I'd heard of a martial arts master practising near my judo club, and now I'd been rewarded with this major achievement.

During the same month that I was awarded the black belt, I also received news that I'd been accepted by the Army to commence training as a Junior Leader in the Royal Corps of Transport, commencing January 1983. My two childhood ambitions had been fulfilled within a month, and I felt amazing. Discipline had always featured heavily in my life whilst growing up, first with my parents, then at primary school, and then with the five years spent studying karate, and it proved to be vital all throughout my military career.

I left juniors and got moved up to the senior karate session, now practising with adult students. I took up my new position in the front row, knowing that all eyes would be on me: here I was, a new black belt surrounded by all these new faces, all desperate to spar with me to see if I was worthy of wearing the belt. It didn't take long before I had gained their respect.

Karate really has been hugely beneficial to me; it's taught me a higher level of discipline and respect – as well as the importance of working hard – and it gave me the confidence to teach lessons, benefiting me later on in my military career. I had been training for over five years, and now it was time to focus on joining the Army. With this in mind, I started preparing to leave my dojo.

Twenty years later, I was standing in a bookshop in London perusing the shelves when one book caught my attention. It was called *Hard Bastards*, and when I opened the first page I saw the words: 'NO WANNABES, NO PANTOMIME GANGSTERS, JUST THE 24 HARDEST MEN IN BRITAIN'. The criteria was based on three qualities: Respect – An attitude of deference, admiration, regard, the state of being honoured. Reputation – A high opinion generally held about a person and, Row – A person who fights and has determination.

I was drawn further and further into the book, and as I started to sift through the pages I was amazed and proud to find a chapter on Shihan. I read the chapter, then took it straight to the counter so I could add it to my book collection.

I felt privileged that I had trained with and been awarded the black belt by Shihan, and I was amazed that the story he'd told me years earlier had now been transcribed into this book. I really appreciated his training regime, particularly how tough it was and the discipline required to advance through the belts, and as I found out, the mindset taught to me by Shihan would prepare me well for my pending basic training.

5

BAPTISM OF FIRE

The 4th January 1983 will forever be rooted in my memory as the date I left home at sixteen to join the Army as a Junior Leader in the Royal Corps of Transport (RCT). I'd applied to join the Army eight months earlier, but had been rejected then due to the MOD halving the amount of vacancies for junior soldiers. In 1982, the United Kingdom had been at war with Argentina over the sovereignty of the Falkland Islands, and in June of that year Port Stanley was liberated, lifting the country, boosting Margaret Thatcher's popularity, and resulting in the biggest influx of young men and women wanting to join the military since World War Two.

I was devastated at being rejected as this had been my long-term ambition and, subsequently, I had no plan B. Failure was not an option, as I wasn't at all interested in staying on at school for A levels, although realistically this wasn't a possibility anyway. I had trained hard for army selection, but had been let down by my poor maths results. I thought this was it, that my army career was on hold or – worst case scenario – over before it had even started, with no other option available to me as I'd put all my time and effort into joining the army. My dad did have a plan B, however, which was paying for extra maths tuition and sending me up to Scotland.

As I had failed the mathematics section of the selection process and was advised by the recruiting sergeant to take on extra study, I enrolled onto an arduous two-week training course in Scotland. Known as the Fort George Volunteers, this was an Army-sponsored exercise developed and led by Lt Colonel

Blashford-Snell, a respected worldwide explorer. So, I commenced private maths lessons and made my way up to Fort William in Scotland less than four weeks after the Falklands War had ended.

I knew that if I could improve my maths score and pass the course, I would be able to secure my place. The course – which consisted of adventure-based training – played into my strengths as it included military skills, team building, hill walking, and water-based activities that culminated in the ascent of Ben Nevis, the highest mountain in the UK standing at 1,345 metres above sea level. Although it was a tough two weeks, the training enabled me to push myself to the fore in all activities and consequently achieve an excellent report. I returned from Scotland full of confidence and immediately retook the entrance exam.

After a two-week wait I was offered a vacancy to join the Junior Leaders Regiment (RCT), commencing in January of 1983. I was informed that the training was extremely tough, as it ran for twelve months to harvest future Non-commissioned Officers (NCOs). Competition would be fierce and high standards would become the standard benchmark. It was also explained to me that if you wanted to get through basic training you must not bring unwanted attention to yourself. The best strategy, therefore, was to become the grey man. You had to make sure you weren't always up the front, but also that you weren't the last; the skill was in blending naturally into the troop.

So, I said goodbye to my mum, sister, and brother, and then jumped into my dad's car with my suitcase for the short journey to the train station before heading for Bath. The journey took about three hours, allowing me plenty of time to contemplate my new life. As I arrived at Bath station I composed myself and stepped onto the platform, where a soldier in ceremonial dress met me and asked for my name. When I replied, I was directed to board a coach full of boys, all sitting in total silence. "Let's go!" shouted the soldier, and that was it – we were driving away from Bath towards my new destination.

As I sat on the coach I experienced a range of emotions; I was feeling nervous, and scared, wondering what would be waiting for me on my arrival. I was leaving the comforts of my own home and entering a whole new world, and I knew from reading books about basic training that I'd have to adapt to military life quickly, which meant having to accept a steep learning curve, with routine and discipline becoming my new norms.

Finally we arrived at the Azimghur Barracks in Colerne, passing the guardroom and pulling up into a large courtyard to be met by a screaming sergeant telling us to grab our belongings. We were then led into our accommodation: a large building with twelve beds per room, each of us being allocated with an individual bed space and locker. This would become our new living space for the foreseeable future. We were told to empty our bags into our lockers, make the beds, and leave any radios and tape recorders in the middle of the room. After that, we were ordered to get changed into the tracksuits that were lying on the beds and then report to the main corridor.

As we stood in line we were told about the coming weeks, including our daily schedule (reveille would be 06.00 and lights out at 22.30), mealtimes, the working day, and expected standards. We were then told to form up on the road adjacent to the accommodation block. By this time the troop sergeant had got changed into a tracksuit and had informed us that we should all be familiar with the joining instructions that had been sent out some three months earlier, which stated that a good level of fitness was a prerequisite for becoming a soldier. With that he told us to turn to the right and commence jogging as a squad. We were directed past the accommodation and past the shop recognised as the NAAFI (Navy, Army, Air Force Institute), being informed that it were out of bounds for the foreseeable future. We were then led out onto the airfield, a massive open space comprising roads, runways, and aircraft hangars. We were given the full tour of the camp, which took about an hour, before returning to our accommodation.

Fortunately, the training programme that my dad had devised and implemented for me had prepared me well. This strict physical training programme consisted of running the streets in all weathers, with ever-increasing distances as my start date drew closer. My strength training came from the many hours I'd spent in the dojo practising karate in preparation for my black belt grading.

Integrating exercise into my daily routine paid dividends as I felt strong sticking with the front runners, and was able to easily pass what would later become our weekly fitness tests.

On that first day we went to the cookhouse for our evening meal, and after dinner we were marched back to our accommodation to find that all our personal radios and tape recorders had been removed. We were instructed to sort out our personal belongings and to get some rest. Lights out occurred at 22.30, leaving me some time to contemplate this Baptism of Fire.

We were woken up at 06.00 the following morning by troop staff crashing bin lids and shouting at the tops of their voices to get out of bed, get washed, and get dressed into our tracksuits. We were then given a lesson in how to make Bed Boxes (a standard military practice of presenting your bed space), and told that this was to become the standard every day. We were marched to the cookhouse for breakfast at 07.00, then straight back to the accommodation for block jobs (cleaning duties). At 08.00 we had to be standing to attention in line for the welcome briefing. We were then allotted our service number and rank. For me it was:

24648251 Junior Driver Baker.

We were also told that we were now part of:

Gloucester Troop, 30 Squadron JLR RCT

It was explained to us that Gloucester Troop would establish itself as champion troop by the end of the first term, no question!

The first week consisted of various briefings, including meeting with the Regimental Sergeant Major (RSM), the one person you did *not* want to end up in front of as he was solely responsible for discipline and inflicting the necessary punishments. We were taught the basics of drill and how to move around in a squad, how to form up on parade, and more physical exercise. We were also introduced to the Basic Fitness Test (BFT), which required a mix of marching at fast pace and running for 1.5 miles in a 30-minute time slot, wearing military clothing. When we got to the 1.5 mile mark we would turn straight around and run back to the start point in a target time of under 15 minutes. By the end of the first term all troop members would be completing the second 1.5 miles in less than 11 minutes, as this would form part of the strategy to become champion troop – something we would later learn was the main objective for the troop staff.

We were introduced to instructors who'd be teaching us military subjects for the term, including drill and turnout, weapon handling, field craft, map & compass, and physical training. I vividly remember the first visit to the gymnasium, which was located a mile from the accommodation. Basically, it was a vast aircraft hangar full of fitness equipment and floor mats. We were met by the PTI (Physical Training Instructor), who was dressed in a smart blue uniform displaying the crossed swords crest on his arm and chest. I was really envious of his job, and knew at that point that I wanted to be a PTI.

At the end of the first week we marched as a squad to the quartermaster to be issued our uniforms. One advantage of having Baker as your surname was that I was always first in line. Yes, my surname definitely had its benefits – that was, apart from when it came to jumping out of a plane five months later. In terms of our uniforms we had already provided our measurements so it was just a case of moving along a line, grabbing the clothing, and placing it into a stuff bag. We were then marched back to the accommodation, issued with marker pens, and told to label every piece of clothing and place them into our lockers. When the following morning arrived we were told to leave the lockers open whilst we went out for another BFT. When we got back to the accommodation we found the contents of all 12 lockers piled on top of each other in the middle of the room, the troop staff stating they trusted we'd labelled up all our personal equipment as instructed the night before.

Making new friends was important as teamwork was critical in the army, so we knew we'd need to bond and make allies quickly. I soon discovered we all had different skill sets, and that by working together and sharing our expertise we'd be able to survive the first few weeks. The first real bond naturally occurred with the person living next to you, and in my case this was a ginger-haired lad from Birmingham who had a similar family background to me and who also loved running. It was good to know that he shared the same emotions and was also nervous about what was lying ahead!

The next important bond was with our roommates, as it soon became apparent that we'd be in competition with the other three rooms of the troop and we didn't want to be branded as the weakest room. This mentality forged strong bonds, but it would also become the cause of some conflict. The training was devised as reward and punishment: you would be rewarded for good performance but would receive punishments for lack of effort or failure to meet the required standard set by troop staff. These punishments included Restriction of Privileges (ROPs) and extra PT being inflicted on all troop members. It would only take one individual to slip up, making them very unpopular with the whole room as the whole troop were punished for their mistakes. This led to people trying to establish themselves as leaders, and quite often, the only way conflict was resolved was by fighting. This naturally led to the law of the jungle being established, where if you were perceived as being weak and not willing to stand up for yourself you could easily become a target, so it was important to establish yourself as not being weak in any way. I had a martial arts background, which I decided to keep as a closely guarded secret.

My mum had taught me about bullies when I was at school, and I kept that lesson in mind during that term. A few years earlier I had upset the school bully, who had decided that he wanted to teach me a lesson; he chased me all the way home and I only just managed to get inside my porch before he caught me, though he stood shouting and screaming at me from the other side of the door. At this point my front door opened and my mum stood there, asking me what was going on. She could tell I was distressed but she showed no sympathy as she told me to go out and face him. With that she opened the porch door and sent me outside to face my nemesis. Needless to say, we traded blows for a few seconds before he turned around and decided to walk away. The next time I saw him we exchanged glares, but he never bothered me again – a valuable lesson learned!

Over the next 11 weeks, basic soldiering skills were the order of the day, every day, in preparation for our passing out at the end of the first term. A good pass result in all military subjects would guarantee passage into the second term and removal of the tag 'NIG' (New Intake Group).

Physical Training (PT) consisted of Recruit and Trained Soldiers PT. Recruit PT was spent inside the gymnasium, undertaking cardiovascular and strength training – now commonly referred to as HITT (High Intensity Interval Training). Over the first term, this consisted of two one-hour sessions per day. Trained Soldiers PT was undertaken outdoors in combat clothing, covering many different disciplines including the infamous log race. This was a team event, where eight men had to carry a telegraph pole weighing 60kg for one mile. There were 16 men assigned to each log, allowing for short rests along the mile-long route. This was a test of teamwork, strength, and fitness, and it pushed everyone to their limits. This race would be the first element in the competition to become champion troop.

The BFT soon became part of daily life, and after six weeks the Combat Fitness Test (CFT) was also introduced. This was a fast-paced march covering eight miles over roads and open terrain while carrying approximately 15kg of equipment, and it was completed as a squad in fighting order, carrying the Self Loading Rifle (SLR) in a time period of less than two hours. Any time over two hours would be a fail.

Another PT staff favourite was milling, which was definitely not for the faint-hearted. This involved two people standing toe to toe, punching each other in the face as furiously as possible for one minute. Unlike boxing, you were not allowed to pause in attacking your opponent and you had to continue until told to stop. This training derives from the arduous selection process for the Parachute Regiment, recognised as 'P Company', its purpose being to replicate conditions of stress and encourage the qualities required in combat situations. The test is seen as a test of determination and fighting spirit. Milling was always preceded with a line out, where you would stand in a long line with the tallest on the right and the shortest on the left, with opponents walking out to fight one another from either end –not good news if you were 5ft 8. If staff decided either party was not giving 100%, you would be made to fight again.

As well as the PT being part of the weekly training syllabus, our troop staff would also have us out in all-weather completing BFTs, log runs, and assault course training in readiness for the end of term champion troop competition.

Troop staff were responsible for drill and turnout for two hours per day on the drill square, going through basic movements and marching until the troop could move as a single unit. Every evening was spent on kit preparation, ensuring we were turned out immaculately and paying particular attention to taking creases out of our uniform, having no dust particles on our clothing, and having spotless bulled boots. Bed Boxes had to be rectangular, and cardboard had to be put into clothing to make it completely square, and then placed in lockers in readiness for inspection. There were weekly inspections, with ROPs issued for not meeting the mandatory standard. ROPs normally consisted of extra guard and cleaning duties, or not being allowed to the NAAFI shop for sweets and fizzy drinks – these items being seen as vital for getting through basic training.

Weapon training in the first term comprised learning to become proficient with the L1A1 SLR, which was capable of semi-automatic fire and had a killing range of 800 metres. Lessons involved learning how to handle and fire the weapon in a safe manner by undertaking a series of competency tasks, leading to the Weapon Handling Test (WHT), which all recruits needed to pass before being allowed to fire the weapon. Once we passed the WHT we were on ranges, with live ammunition firing at targets up to distances of 300 metres.

During that first term, an important element of the training syllabus was field craft, as this would shape your journey to becoming a competent soldier. The basic elements of field craft are learning to fight and survive, personal administration, and being an asset to your commander. Fieldcraft took place outdoors, which proved tough as it was still winter and there was snow on the ground. At the end of January we were sent out on the first two-day exercise to Salisbury Plain, where we were taught the basics of fieldcraft. Tactical fieldcraft exercises simulate combat situations where enemy forces are present or pose a serious threat. The other squadrons would act as the enemy forces.

We were dropped off by coach at the corner of the training area while it was still daylight, and then had to move as a rifle patrol in a series of formations dependent on the country we were crossing. After a two-hour walk we got to the location where we would lay up for the night. Camp admin included standard routine and setting sentries (guards to protect the camp) at strategic points, ensuring that the triangular formation of the camp location was protected from all angles should we come under attack from enemy forces. Taking on hot food and drink was deemed critical, so this was the first task to complete once the location was secure. Cooking in the field meant using a small metal cooker filled with hexamine fuel blocks, and filling a mess tin with water in order to cook the varied menu items on offer from the rations pack (the rat pack). There were a number of different menu choices, but we were always happy to receive the box that came with the Mars Bar – guaranteed to give you that instant sugar boost.

Once the cooking was underway it would be time to build your basha (shelter), which was a single waterproof sheet that would – if constructed properly – protect you from the elements. Once done it was personal admin, sleeping bag out, and kit check (including rifle), and then it was time to get the scoff (food) down your neck. We were given sentry duties throughout the night and told to go to sleep if not on sentry duty.

We were woken up before sunrise and told to get into all round defence to protect the location. It was absolutely freezing, with frost all over the ground, so when the sunrise came it was a welcome comfort, allowing a small feeling of warmth to return to our shivering bodies. The following day we were taught skills including more camp routine, camouflage and concealment, judging distances, and target recognition. The coach picked us up early afternoon, allowing us some much-needed sleep on the way back to Colerne.

The final week of term was spent competing in competitions that would define champion troop, permitting the winners to wear red and white epaulettes on their ceremonial uniform. When we weren't competing, time would be spent on the drill square, perfecting marching preparations in readiness for the passing out parade. This would take place in front of our parents, and would allow us passage into the second term.

Waiting at the start line dressed in full combat clothing, we knew maximum effort would secure a win in the log race. We were up against two other squadrons, but had gained advantage by spending many hours preparing for this moment.

"Pick up the log!" shouted the PTI. *"Stand by!"* Go!"

With that we were off on the mile-long course. We set off at a great pace, and as we approached the first 100 metres I shouted out, *"Prepare to change!"* giving notice to the other troop members who were running beside us to take up their positions on the log.

"Change!"

They smashed into us, taking up position on the log for the next 100 metres as we continued to run parallel, offering encouragement until it was time to return to the log to us. Although we got to the halfway point first, we knew that the next 0.5 miles would be decisive, so we continued with pace and it wasn't long before we were crossing the finish line in first place – job done! We were awarded additional points for the determination, aggression, and leadership we'd shown during the race.

Gloucester Troop also smashed the BFT, drill and assault course competitions, thus allowing all troop members to wear red and white epaulettes after being crowned Champion Troop – something that had been unquestionably programmed into our mindset from day one!

The final day of term eventually came, and it was time to pass out. We formed up on the main parade square in ceremonial dress (Number 2s), our troop wearing our new red and white epaulettes, and then – formed up in three squadrons – we marched up to the Main Drill Hangar, where VIPs and parents were eagerly awaiting our entry. We marched in as trained soldiers, having left home three months earlier as inexperienced sixteen-year-olds.

Gloucester Troop started out with 42 recruits, but numbers had reduced down to 32 by the end of April. The training had been ruthless –much harder than anyone had anticipated – and the next term would be just as hard. Even so, it was my aim to still be a member of Gloucester Troop by the end of term two. I was determined.

6

SOLDIERING ON

My four weeks of leave was time well spent with family, enjoying the freedoms of civilian life with some much-needed and well-earned downtime. I caught up with friends, and I also went back to karate to retain some routine. I felt like a changed man; having just gone through three months of rigorous training, I'd returned to find that nothing had changed at home. My friends were all caught up in the same old routine of work followed by pub followed by work... and so on.

I arrived back at Colerne early May to be told that I'd been promoted to Lance Corporal and would therefore become part of a training team responsible for the new recruits arriving a few days later. I had now become the Soldier at Bath Railway Station, dressed smartly in Number 2s and directing brand new recruits to the coach for the short journey back to barracks. This promotion would get me away from troop routine and it also offered additional responsibilities, though my focus would still remain on passing out at the end of term. Some things were the same as before, while some things were slightly different. For instance, all radios and tape recorders removed in January had been given back, allowing some familiarity to return.

After moving into my new accommodation, I got ready to receive the recruits who would no doubt be in the same frame of mind I'd been in some four months before. My job was to mentor them whilst they adapted to military life.

During the first week of term the troop got called to a meeting to be informed that all personnel would be participating in a parachute jump from 3,500 feet. We were given two weeks' notice to prepare, then taken out onto the airfield to commence a day-long course. This consisted of familiarisation and fitting of the parachute equipment, aircraft drills – including exiting in a safe, stable body position – and controlling and landing the parachute canopy. The rest of the time was spent learning how to identify malfunctions and how to operate the reserve parachute.

Eventually, four of us climbed inside the small Cessna aircraft with the Jump Master. The jump order would be alphabetical, giving me no option but to be the first troop member to exit the aircraft – no pressure, then! I was nervous, but at least going out first would get it over with quickly, leaving no time for quiet contemplation. As we approached 3,500 feet, the Jump Master told me to prepare to jump, which necessitated climbing out onto the wing and launching myself backwards into the air, arching my body on his command: "GO!"

Before I knew it, I was falling.

One Thousand

Two Thousand

Three Thousand

Check Canopy

The canopy opened after a few seconds and I found myself descending towards the Drop Zone, hoping to hit the landing site. My sense of fear had changed to calm once the opening checks were complete and I was flying under canopy. Fortunately I managed to steer within a few feet of the landing site, where the other troop members were eagerly awaiting their turn. I felt ecstatic; I'd done it, and I could now relax while watching everyone else make their jumps.

A new obligation for the second term was participating in a hobby over two evenings a week – allowing no time for boredom to settle – and I decided on gymnastics as I enjoyed time spent in the gymnasium and wanted to join the Regimental Gymnastics Team. The training regime was hard; it involved learning a series of gymnastic skills over a high vault in a set routine in a team. This team consisted of 30 individuals, lined up in three rows, who would take it in turns to run at the vault at high speed and jump onto a small trampoline positioned in front of the vault, gaining the correct height in order to clear it. We entered the vault from three different starting points, one after the other, with split second timing between entering and leaving the vault. The skills we had to learn started off basic, becoming increasingly harder until the final skills were technically difficult, allowing no room for error.

By the end of the term I would be competing in the JLR Gymnastics Display Team in army competitions all around the country and at local community events. I also got to spend a weekend at the Army School of Physical Training (ASPT) in Aldershot, which gave me a really good insight into life as a PTI and made me even more determined to attend the course so I could wear the ASPT cap badge. The icing on the cake came when we had to put on a display at the end of term – in front of VIPs and parents – and were awarded the Regimental Colours for overall commitment and effort.

Physical training continued at pace, both with PTIs and the troop sergeant. BFT and CFT times were getting faster and faster, with everyone making the 11-minute mark for the BFT and the two-hour target for the CFT. Log runs and assault course timings were improving all the time and my body shape was changing fast; I was now fitter and stronger than I'd ever been before.

Military discipline had been founded on drill, which had been proven time and time again in battle, and had now become pivotal during the second term. We spent hours on the drill square perfecting advanced moves, including rifle and ceremonial drill and taking it in turns to act as the drill sergeant, shouting out words of commands and drilling the troop. Doing drill well demanded precision, effort, and fully tested individual alertness and control. We practised until we could all move as one individual unit, and we were proud to march around camp holding our heads high, full of confidence.

Skill at Arms continued with two of the most famous weapon systems used by the British Army: the 9mm Submachine Gun (SMG), and the Light Machine Gun (LMG) – or Bren Gun as it was more commonly known. The Sterling submachine gun was tested during 1944, but it didn't come into full service until 1953, when it was proven to be a reliable weapon. The SMG remained in service until 1994, being used in many conflicts including Aden, Vietnam, and Northern Ireland. The Bren Gun was made in Britain during the 1930s and was widely used in all major conflicts around the world, including World War Two, the Falklands, and the Gulf War. It remained in service until 2006.

I'd grown up playing with action men who had these very weapons at their disposal, I was really happy to finally get my hands on them. I found it unbelievable that these weapons, which predated the Second World War, were still in active service in 1983, but they were still reliable, well tested, and proven. We were trained in readiness for Battle Camp, which was looming, and which was recognised as the most important and challenging phase of the term. It was aimed at testing both our basic and advanced soldiering skills.

NBC warfare – (Nuclear, Biological, and Chemical), which was deemed a real threat during the Cold War – was soon introduced as part of the fieldcraft syllabus. During battle, there was a heightened risk of a chemical attack, so training was critical as our first priority was first to survive the NBC strike, and then still be capable of fighting. We were therefore issued with individual protective equipment, were trained in its use, and were taught what to do in the immediate aftermath of any attack. When the threat was imminent we would be dressed in NBC clothing and drilled in the chemical safety rule, 'Be in Time, Mask in Nine,' meaning you had nine seconds to put on the respirator (gas mask). Once trained, we were given a taste (literally) of a chemical attack in the form of CS gas in the gas chamber.

So, we got changed into our NBC clothing and were called into the chamber, where we started walking around in a clockwise direction, unaware that CS tablets were being lit in the corner of the room. Soon enough, smoke started to fill the small space, and the instructor shouted out, "Gas, Gas, Gas!"

With that we completed the full drills:

Eyes closed
Stop breathing
Stand with back to smoke
Respirator on
Blow out hard, shout out, 'Gas, Gas, and Gas!' and then breathe normally.

Once our clothing had been fully checked by the instructors, basic drills were completed, ensuring our masks were functioning correctly. After a few minutes we were told to remove our masks individually, and then we had to try answering questions starting with our name, rank, and number.

Baker
Junior Lance Corpo…
246…

I trailed off, coughing profusely, my eyes streaming and a nauseous feeling in my stomach. I was quickly led outside, and even with the fresh air making its way to my lungs the symptoms lasted 10 minutes or so. It was a really dreadful feeling; the worst ever, in fact! A harsh introduction to chemical warfare.

The troop sergeant's primary job was to turn teenagers into fully trained soldiers, who would then be ready to join operational units anywhere in the world. He had a tough exterior, and he saw part of his role as having to 'bin' (a military term meaning 'to get rid') weak recruits by breaking individuals that he felt weren't up to his standard. He did this by various means. He would show little empathy for any troop member who did not meet his standard, and he would not hesitate in getting rid of them. It seemed he would take turns in targeting individuals to see how far they were able to go before they gave up and wanted to leave, testing their resilience to the full. My turn didn't come until midway through the second term, by which time at least 12 individuals had already left the troop.

I was on a fieldcraft weekend at the time, and I felt like he begrudged me for having a different life with another troop – one that came with a number of perks. He called me aside and told me that I wasn't applying myself completely to the training syllabus. He then decided to make my life hell for the entire weekend, singling me out all the time and culminating in making me carry all my personal equipment – including a fully loaded magazine box for the LMG, weighing in excess of 20kg. This was made even harder as this element of the exercise included a chemical attack threat, resulting in NBC suits having to be worn over our standard combat clothing. Even so, I fought on, knowing that I couldn't let him beat me like he'd done with the other recruits before me.

During my first term I'd had several conversations with my mum about wanting to leave when I was feeling low, and she'd always given me the same advice: if I wanted to leave she would fully support my decision, but I shouldn't leave because of the troop sergeant. "Make it your choice," she'd tell me, "not his!" Besides, I'd been in this type of situation before whilst practising karate under the Shihan, who expected the highest of standards and would always push me, resulting in me becoming a stronger karateka. I knew I could do it, and I knew I wouldn't let it break me.

After the weekend I went back to my recruit troop, ensuring that the recruits continued to learn and gain passes in all military subjects. My troop staff backed off, so I hoped that the time of targeting me had passed, allowing me time to prepare for the imminent adventure training week.

We left Colerne for Penhale Training Camp (located on the outskirts of Newquay) to undertake adventurous training (AT), which felt like a bit of respite as it allowed time away from soldiering, and gave us the chance to wear civvies (civilian clothing) for the week. We turned up late Saturday afternoon and had the evening to ourselves, allowing us to enjoy some time in the NAAFI. The following morning was taken up with lectures from the AT staff, followed by a coastal walk, and then we were given the afternoon off. The troop sergeant, however, had other ideas; he took us all out on a two-hour run around the country roads of Penhale, proving that even though we were away from the barracks he was still in charge and we were soldiers first!

Adventure training develops courage, leadership, and effective teamwork by placing you outside your comfort zone, by creating challenging adventurous activities, and by providing controlled exposure to risk, allowing teams to bond quickly. By now the troop had bonded well, with friendships established and enemies made, which was natural and which would become the standard for the remaining time spent at Colerne. I really enjoyed AT, having experienced it earlier with the Fort George Volunteers in Scotland. Although AT was less regimented, discipline was still at the core of all the activities, as failing to listen to instructions or ignoring orders could have severe consequences. We were warned, for instance, that a boy who'd failed to follow instructions had been back termed after he fell down a cliff the previous year, suffering a broken leg!

The week consisted of Coasteering, which entails moving along the intertidal zone (area above sea) by foot without any aids along long areas of coastline, which meant climbing and scrambling over precarious rock formations, trying to stay out of the water. This was challenging, but it was great fun watching individuals falling into the sea and then having to swim to a good point of entry to scale up the cliffs and rejoin the group. We also undertook sea kayaking, learning to ride the high waves. This was great fun, with more time being spent in the sea than in the kayaks due to everyone capsizing on a regular basis.

The climbing and abseiling phase was spent on a number of rock formations along the coastline, with great views overlooking the sea. Here we were taught basic rope work, learning how to act as a safety anchor for your partner. One would climb whilst the other climber would stay on the ground, releasing the rope, allowing them to control the ascent and to stop any falls. The climbs started out easy and progressively got harder. Once at the top of the rock face you would enjoy the view for a few seconds before abseiling back down to where your climbing partner was waiting. The day was spent swapping between climbing and acting as belay (safety person). The last day finished with a full day at surfing school that took place on the famous Cornish beaches – this was a great way to end a superb week of AT, plus it added a brand new skill set to my portfolio.

The next week we spent hours preparing for the block inspection that would be undertaken by the Officer Commanding (OC), where anything short of perfection would be a failure. The inspection included all living accommodation, personal bed space, everything inside your locker, the washrooms, and all corridors. This was solely intended to get us all back into military mode after our week of AT, and standards were really high. We were now halfway through the second term and there was no room for complacency; the windows and mirrors had to be spotless, the sanitary ware gleaming, and all floors highly polished so that you could see your own reflection in them. All bed boxes had to be symmetrical with each other and all lockers had to display all personal equipment in unison. When the OC entered the room we were called to attention, and I saluted him as he approached my bed space, where we exchanged pleasantries.

Once the inspection was over it was judged by the troop sergeant that we had failed, as it was not up to the expected standard. With that he told us to get changed into combat trousers, t-shirts, and boots, and parade on the road. He informed us that he was going to take us on the 'shit run', running and crawling through muddy fields and streams for just under an hour before returning back to the block. He then informed everyone that we had one hour to clean the clothing we were wearing in readiness to be inspected again. Looking back, this was an impossible task, given that there were no washing or drying machines available, but we all tried our best and formed back up on the road, eagerly awaiting his return. Yet again the troop failed the inspection and we were all put on show parade for twenty-four hours. This consists of turning up at the Guard Room at 6.00 a.m. in Number 2s and being inspected by the Guard Commander. If it was deemed that you were not immaculately turned out, you would have to report back on the hour every hour until you had met the standard. If called back you would turn up in a different uniform decided by the Guard Commander. Needless to say, the majority of the troop were still being inspected past 6.00 p.m. and a few went on to 10.00 p.m. – it was a real test of grit!

7

FAILURE, NOT AN OPTION

Battle Camp was upon us: a full week designed to test our soldiering skills – basic/advanced fieldcraft, survival, and shooting – on the battlefield, ending with a three-day exercise. This test was crucial; if we didn't meet the standard, it would prevent passage to the final term.

The first two days of Battle Camp were spent on the ranges, firstly zeroing the SLR and then firing it. Zeroing the weapon involved firing sets of five rounds at certain targets to align the sights until the shots were deemed accurate, and on target. Once zeroed, we fired the remainder of the rounds from the allotted magazines, then waited patiently for the butt party (at the target location point) to count the confirmed hits and to feed back the results. News travelled fast that we had all passed the Annual Personal Weapons Test (APWT).

The second day's undertaking of the APWT featured both the SMG and LMG. I had just finished firing the LMG when the instructor shouted out, "Stop firing!" followed by, "Unload!" I carried out the drills as taught... and BANG! A round went flying down the range. I had a negligent discharge (ND), which by definition is a discharge of a firearm involving culpable carelessness – in military terms, a chargeable offence. Any accidental discharge is negligent under the assumption that a soldier should have full control of his rifle at all times.

"Shit," I whispered under my breath. I had totally messed up; I'd actually handed the troop sergeant his trump card, allowing him to get rid of me, if he so chose. I was devastated – this could see me back termed, thrown out. I was convinced that I'd followed the correct drills, but unfortunately for me it was an ND, so there was no debate to be had.

I woke up the following morning absolutely distraught with all my confidence gone, which wasn't ideal considering the tough day I had ahead of me. Firstly, I had to go through basic fieldcraft testing, finishing with 'Close Quarter Battle' (CQB) drills, which necessitated going through derelict buildings searching for and engaging enemy forces. I managed to hold it together for the morning, but the more I thought about what had happened on the ranges the more anxious I became, and any tiny bit of confidence I had left disappeared fast.

I got called forward to the CQB alongside another troop member, as this test was done in pairs. We were then given our briefing, stating that there were known enemies and friendly forces in the area and, therefore, we would have to clear the buildings one by one, ensuring we didn't take any civilian casualties. We headed straight out towards the village.

As we approached the first building my mind was totally elsewhere, not at all on the job, and considering my delayed reaction to enemy fire, the Directing Staff (DS) walking behind me could sense my distraction. I also forgot the drills and subsequently got pulled out. Things had now gone from bad to worse, my negativity having beaten me completely. Consequently, I was informed that I had failed, but that I would have another chance to pass the CQB at the end of Battle Camp.

This was the first time I had been well and truly beaten, simply by allowing negativity to get the better of me. I was to be given a second chance, though – meaning I had not received a straight fail – which was at least some positive news for me to bank, I thought! The consequences of failing Battle Camp were enormous, and I was now staring that failure right in the face. I had to act fast, by overcoming adversity, by stopping making excuses for my performance, and by refocusing my mindset. The key for me was not to focus on what had happened, but instead to concentrate on how I was going to respond – I had one choice to make, and I was going to make the right decision. I now had to make sure I passed this course. The consequences of failure were far too important.

Kit packed and checked, ammunition and rations issued, rifles cleaned and lightly lubricated, and orders received. Once we were ready, we were loaded into the back of a truck in our fighting patrols to go out on exercise. When we arrived at a track leading into a wooded area we jumped off, with all our personal equipment to hand. We also had the grid reference to the first location, where we would set up our defensive positions. I was part of a nine-person fighting patrol, with three fighting patrols in total, and known enemy forces in the area. The first patrol left to perform a reconnaissance of the first location, ensuring it was safe to enter, whilst we held back until news came through that it was safe to proceed. After a 90-minute walk across various terrains, we approached the location to meet the forward troop.

"Halt!"

"Hands Up."

"Advance One, and be recognised."

"Lima, Lima," the sentry stated.

"X-ray, Delta," replied the point man.

Passwords were exchanged, confirming that friendly forces were entering the location, already fortified by the first patrol. Sentries had also been set, allowing us time to get on with camp routine. The first job consisted of working in pairs, constructing a fire trench and providing vital cover from enemy fire. This was not an easy task, having to dig a large trench capable of protecting two people. The section commander set out defensive positions, ensuring that all-round cover was provided. Arcs of fire agreed, trip flares set, then it was time to eat and sleep, our brief: to hold and protect the location from enemy forces. By that point we had been on the go for most of the day, allowing no time for any negativity to set in. In fact, the reverse was starting to happen: I had managed to refocus my thoughts on passing Battle Camp, and my confidence was returning fast.

The next 48 hours were spent being tested in advanced fieldcraft, including patrolling at night, having to adapt to the different conditions that darkness brings, and movement, noise, and vision whilst out on reconnaissance patrols. Once back at the location we undertook sentry duties and carried on with standard camp routine, getting sleep when we could.

The location came under enemy attack just before sunrise on the final day. We were in 'all-round defence' when enemy forces were spotted advancing towards our location, at which point we came under fire. We stood tall in the trenches, returning fire at the enemy with thunder flashes and smoke grenades going off all around us. Everything was chaotic – lots of noise, the air filled with dark smoke, and the constant noise of enemy fire on top of us – but we defended our position and stood fast. Eventually, it was over. We had managed to hold our ground, not allowing it to fall into enemy hands, and therefore had fulfilled the key objective.

We regrouped before checking on casualties and ammunition etc. Then we had to fill in the trenches, pack up our kit, and litter sweep before heading off in single file back to the drop-off point.

My confidence had now returned in spades, and I felt ready to undertake the CQB once again. This time I responded to enemy fire and cleared all houses as instructed, killing the enemy and protecting the civilians. I received a full pass mark.

Being so close to failure had felt horrible, and I'd known that my immediate future was dependent on focusing my mindset and clawing back the confidence I'd previously lost. By changing my mindset I gained a pass mark for Battle Camp and achieved passage into the third term, although this did come with one caveat: the ND issue, which was likely to be a discussion point at the start of the third term.

After competing in the Regimental Display Team at the end of term parade, we were sent off on our four-week leave during the summer of 1983. The end of term brief, given by the troop sergeant, reminded us all to stay disciplined whilst on leave as we were subject to both English and Military Law, reminding us that any incidents that occurred while on leave would be dealt with by the RSM (Regimental sergeant major) on our return. We were also warned to maintain our fitness levels, as there would be an endurance test awaiting us all when we got back.

8

SMASHING IT

I travelled home and quickly met up with friends, catching up on news and what they'd all been doing. My dad worked for British Airways, allowing concessionary air travel, meaning that I got to spend seven days in Mallorca and a further ten days in Greece, giving me some quality time with my family. I also made sure to heed the warning given to me before my leave: I maintained my fitness levels by running long distances in Mallorca, Greece, and back at home.

I arrived back in Colerne late August and returned to my troop accommodation to start preparations for my JMQC (Junior Military Qualification Certificate) training, a five-week course that would qualify me for future promotion in the Army. This course was available if you passed preselection, and was part and parcel of Junior Leader training, harvesting the future NCOs. It involved being tested on all elements of military training, as well as the ability to teach lessons. The course would include inspections, competition, punishment and plenty of bullshit, something that I had become well accustomed to!

We were now top of the food chain – the tag 'NIG' a distant memory, having been replaced by 'Sweat' (experienced soldier) – and all eyes were on our troop as we had already survived two arduous terms. As promised, our fitness was tested the second week back by participating in a 17-mile run. Well, it was actually an organised sponsored walk, but our instructions were that it had to be undertaken as a run and that everyone had to finish!

The ND had not been mentioned, so I kept my head down and put all my effort into the run, staying at the front with the troop sergeant and finishing in the top three, gaining some much-needed praise. Not everybody was so lucky; two troop members failed to finish, with the troop sergeant stating that, "They did not maintain their fitness levels as instructed," so a group punishment would now be imminent.

During the five-day selection process for the JMQC, all troop members participated in a number of test phases: physical training, weapon handling, and drill practice, followed by inspection, inspection, inspection.

I was advised that I had passed selection and would be commencing the following week alongside ten other successful candidates. Troop promotions were also publicised, but as expected I missed out, blaming the ND.

I had received both good and bad news on the same day. I felt totally elated at being put forward for the JMQC, and passing selection boosted my confidence tenfold as only the best members were put forward, confirming that I was a competent soldier. It was, however, a double-edged sword, as other successful candidates had all received their promotions. Still, I couldn't let this get the better of me.

Later in my military career a similar situation would come back to bite me, but for very different reasons.

I spent the next few days preparing for the course, moving into new accommodation and bonding with the other 10 members. Teamwork would be more critical now than ever, as we would need to bond quickly and work as one. This was going to be the final hard test of the term as, once completed, we would move into the final phase of training. This phase was considered the most enjoyable as it included adventure training, and motorbike and car driver training.

A successful pass would allow me to join any operational unit, with a highly regarded professional qualification.

Week One

We spent all weekend making sure the accommodation was spotless, ironing our uniforms, and sorting out our lockers in preparation for the first week. The inspection didn't go well, however, and was deemed below standard, resulting in everyone being put on show parade. There were more inspections, followed by further show parades, as well as revision periods covering drill, skill at arms, map reading, and PT. Eventually, we survived the first week unscathed and started preparing for week two.

Week Two

Déjà vu – in week two we failed the inspection and were put on show parade again! We were also introduced to 'Method of Instruction' (MOI) and how to teach lessons. Passing this course required three good teaching passes, using the acronym EDIP:

Explain
Demonstrate
Imitate
Practice

Week Three

Déjà vu again, with another failed inspection! During this week I started lesson planning and teaching practices. My first skill at arms lesson and the introduction to the SLR went well, and this was soon followed by my drill lesson, during which my turnings on the march went badly; I was brought back to reality by the drill sergeant's critique. I carried on trawling through the lessons, as we wouldn't know what we'd be teaching until the day of the test, so I had to become competent in all drill and skill at arms lessons.

Week Four

Yes, you guessed it: another failed inspection. As it transpired, we were always going to fail the first four weeks regardless of what we did, as this was simply the process. We continued teaching lessons and being tested, successfully passing map and compass. We then deployed for the exercise where our fieldcraft skills would be tested. My role as section commander challenged me, as I took charge of the section just at the point where we came under attack, consequently having to 'Bug Out' (leave location) and move to a Rendezvous Point (RV) under tactical conditions.

Week Five

Incredibly, we passed the last inspection, so there was no show parade for the first time in five weeks! We were now into test week, which commenced with physical training comprising BFT and CTFs, assault course, and log run. I taught the 'Load, Unload, and Ready' drills for the SLR and smashed it, meaning that I only had the drill teaching practice left.

Immaculately turned out, dressed in number 2s on the parade square, 11 troop members waited for the RSM to turn up to carry out the inspection. It was vital that we all passed. We were called out individually, marched out to the drill sergeant, and were informed which lesson we were going to teach to the squad.

"Baker!"

I came to attention, then marched out to the drill sergeant to receive my lesson.

"The Right Turn at the Halt."

I marched back, composed myself, and turned to the squad in readiness to commence the lesson.

"Taking you a stage further in your foot drill, I am now going to teach you the right turn at the halt," I informed them. "The reason this movement is taught is to enable you as an individual – or when in a body of men – to move through an angle of 90 degrees to the right in a smart, uniform, and soldier-like manner. On the command, stand easy, look this way, and I will give you a complete demonstration of the movement."

"*Stand easy!*"

"Relax and look this way!"

I then demonstrated the movement by shouting out, "*Right turn!*" (followed by the timings).

"There you saw a complete demonstration of the movement," I continued. "For the purpose of instruction, this movement is broken down into parts, each part being numbered. Continue to look this way and I will demonstrate the action to be carried out on receipt of the word of command."

"Turning by numbers, *Right turn one!*"

"*Immediately* on receiving the word of command, the head, shoulders, body, and right foot are forced through an angle of 90 degrees to the right, by pivoting on the heel of my right foot and the ball of my left foot. I then freeze in this position."

"Points to note: the right foot is flat and firm on the ground. My body weight is over the right foot. Both knees are braced and the remainder of my body is erect and square to the front. Are there any questions?"

The lesson was moved on by the drill sergeant to final practice, and I was then told to stop and rejoin the squad. After the final troop member had completed his drill lesson we were all dismissed and told to go back to our accommodation. The JMQC was over and we could now start thinking about the final phase of training, commencing with AT.

The adventure training was a welcome break after finishing the JMQC, as it was a full week away from drill, skill at arms, PT, and relentless inspections. We were based in Somerset, where we undertook hill walking, rock climbing, mountain biking, and water-based activities including canoeing, kayaking, and sailing. This was the perfect way to wind down after a gruelling five weeks, with all troop members coming back together for our remaining time at Colerne. Towards the end of the week we were informed of the JMQC results, being told that there was only one failure. I was pleased to hear that I would be leaving Junior Leaders with a well-recognised qualification – a massive turnaround considering that, just a few weeks earlier, I had been standing in the holding area on Battle Camp ready to undertake the CQB, totally drained of all confidence.

Now, the Gucci training phase was about to commence: a two-week motorbike training course starting with Phase 1 training on and around the airfield, with the second week involving us leaving camp and driving around Box, Bath, and Chippenham. This was excellent and well worth the wait, with time spent on the open roads, and regular rest stops where we got to sample the local cuisine in roadside cafes. The course concluded with the full test, and I successfully passed both Parts 1 and 2, receiving my full bike licence. This was followed by a three-week intensive car driver training course (three to a car), again starting on the airfield and then moving on to the open roads around Somerset. I'd passed my driving test by the middle of week three on my first attempt, way before many of my friends back home did, so I was really chuffed. Holding both licences by the age of seventeen was a great achievement, and on the back of the JMQC my mindset was really strong, my confidence running high.

It was now December 1983 and we were coming towards the end of basic training. The troop sergeant had been posted to another unit, so was no longer around. The soundtrack of the year was Michael Jackson's *Thriller* (which had been released in 1982), with the key anthems for the year being *Billie Jean*, *Beat It*, and *Thriller* itself.

A significant moment for the troop was watching the *Thriller* video late at night (we had access to a television by then) in complete darkness, as it was past lights out and we would have been punished if caught! It was a brilliant video and it really was the soundtrack of the year; we all listened to it during the second and third terms, giving us all a much-needed boost.

9

ALMOST THERE

The last year had pushed me to my limits. I remember being warned by the recruiting sergeant that tough training, fierce competition, and high standards would become the new benchmarks, and he wasn't wrong: the training had been brutal, with many recruits not even making it through to the final term. I had prepared well by arriving fit and well disciplined, but I wasn't ready for the inspection regime, the show parades, or the constant attention to detail. I had also yielded advice on maintaining a low profile and trying not to bring any unwanted attention my way.

Having left home at sixteen I had to grow up fast, especially as I was immediately thrown into this completely alien world where life was going to be so different to what I'd been used to. There was plenty to learn whilst living under constant assessment, in an environment of reward and punishment. The training was certainly effective, turning adolescent boys into young men over just a twelve-month period. Like school, I got through it unscathed, by achieving the desired standard, passing basic training, winning champion troop, being awarded regimental colours, passing both driving tests, and – the *icing on the cake* – attaining the Junior Military Qualification Certificate. This was my baptism of fire, but the important lessons I learnt would go on to become my genetic footprint.

In January 1984 I was posted to Driffield, Yorkshire to join 32 Squadron. We were still junior leaders, but now we were also the crème de la crème of the regiment, having successfully completed basic training. This was going to be a very different environment, with no locker inspections, drill, or physical training; now the emphasis was on learning the relevant skills in readiness to join the operational units. We also had the freedom to travel out of camp to towns like Scarborough, Bridlington, and Hull.

We were transported daily to the 'Army School of Mechanical Transport', based at Leconfield, to be taught the basic vehicles of the army – car, Land Rover, and the 4-tonne HGV truck – in readiness to qualify.

On our arrival at the Army School, we were directed to a hangar to receive a briefing from the Officer Commanding. I remember his welcome speech, in which he stated that the real work was just about to commence, with this next phase being far more important than the time we'd spent at Colerne. He warned everyone that we'd soon be out on the roads in military vehicles, stating that this came with responsibility and asserting that "these vehicles were as dangerous as a loaded rifle when not treated with respect".

We then met our instructors who introduced us to the first vehicle, a Vauxhall Chevette estate, starting off on the airfield before heading out of camp towards Hull. As I'd only passed my test some two months earlier, I felt a little nervous. Then I was introduced to the short wheel base Land Rover to be taught the skills of 'off-road' driving. The off-road course was sited behind camp and consisted of challenging man-made and natural features. We were taught how to overcome step ascents followed by sharp descents, water gullies, mud-filled holes, and difficult terrain.

After the first week we got introduced to the weekly disco held on camp, allowing interaction with the local girls on a regular basis. If I thought competition at school was fierce, this was a whole different level. Thirty girls would come into camp and would have 120 adolescent men to choose from. I was still shy so had no success at the discos, but those who were successful were restricted by camp rules; there would be no looming relationships here.

70

HGV driver training commenced with the Bedford TK, a basic military truck. I got off to a good start but I didn't like the instructor's methods; he was a retired RSM who was convinced he was still serving. He would treat the lessons in the same way as he would drilling a squad, with constant shouting and swearing. As well as this, a particularly hard section of the test included reversing the vehicle into a set position, which proved a difficult manoeuvre to learn.

The instructor's constant shouting resulted in me losing all confidence and not enjoying the driver training one bit. It even got to the stage where I was no longer concentrating on the driving but more on his comments. I was just starting to stare failure in the face, however, when a change in circumstances brought a new instructor to the table – fortunately, my instructor had gone off sick, allowing a replacement to be found. With just this one simple change, my mindset immediately transformed and my confidence was restored. This time I was given encouragement, and was spoken to rather than shouted at. I managed to master the reversing manoeuvre and was put forward for my test, passing first time. I was ecstatic, especially as just a couple of weeks earlier I'd been starting to doubt my own ability.

With the test completed, I was now into the final phase: familiarisation with the Bedford MK, the standard military off-road truck. This involved taking it on and off-road, making the next few days the best.

We were then introduced to brand new military hardware straight from the factory floor: the Bedford TM 4x4 vehicle, an 8-tonne flatbed cargo truck designed to carry standard NATO ammunition as well as being a troop carrier. It was fitted with an ATLAS self-loading hydraulic crane located behind the cab, allowing the operator to work independently when loading and unloading supplies. The driver's cab had a really cool roof hatch with fixings for a light machine gun to be mounted, which also doubled up as an observation point. These vehicles were turbocharged, capable of four-wheel drive, and benefitted from power-assisted steering, something military vehicles had been missing to date. They had been tested to destruction, proving they were the perfect match for the military.

We spent five days familiarising ourselves and playing with these new toys, driving all over Yorkshire in convoy fashion, heading out early morning and returning late afternoon. They were very different from the TK and MK, with the power-assisted steering making them feel so much lighter than the previous vehicles. The other noticeable difference was the speed and acceleration, particularly when the turbocharger kicked in.

This concluded my time in junior leaders, from January 1983 to April 1984. I was now ready to join my operational unit, having received my posting to Minden, West Germany.

Transferable skills - Always the Gymnast

Childhood ambition achieved – Awarded Black Belt 1st Dan

Getting ready for the weekly locker Inspection –
Failure had consequences

Ready to Jump – First out the door

River Crossing - It was essential to keep our clothing bags dry

Happy - Motorbike test complete

End of term parade - Champion Troop –
wearing red and white epaulettes with pride

West Germany - waiting to be called forward

East meets West - Russian Sector (East Berlin)

Heading South – The Sahara awaits

Captured Vehicle – Falkland Islands

Medical Cover – Belize

10

TWO TRIBES

The charts during this time were dominated by Frankie Goes to Hollywood and their controversial song, *Relax*, which had reached number 6 after the band performed it on *Top of the Pops* in January 1984. Radio 1 disc jockey, Mike Reid, refused to play it, citing his dislike for both the lyrics and the record sleeve. Less than three weeks later, however, it had propelled to the number 1 spot. The video for the band's next single, *Two Tribes*, was then released and depicted a wrestling match between then-US President Ronald Regan and then-Soviet General Secretary Konstantin Chernenko in front of world leaders, symbolising the Cold War and depicting the nuclear threat. *Two Tribes* also made it to the number 1 spot, reviving further interest for *Relax*.

The song was timely, as I'd been posted to the 4th Armoured Division – located in Minden, West Germany – to serve in the British Army of the Rhine (BAOR). I thought back to those school assemblies where I'd learnt all about the threat of nuclear war, and here I was now, living in Germany and protecting Western Europe from the potential menace of the time, the Soviet Union. The second BAOR was formed in August 1945, commanded by Field Marshal Montgomery in order to control the British zone of occupied Germany.

Thirty fresh soldiers – new arrivals made up from trained soldiers exiting junior leaders, and adult soldiers (classified eighteen at point of entry) – had just completed 10 weeks of basic training at Aldershot, and were fittingly named 'ten week wonders'. We reported to the guard commander, who welcomed us before directing us to our temporary accommodation. My first impression was that the camp was massive, as there were vast areas of concrete standings, with rows and rows of military hardware, buildings, and accommodation blocks. This was now my home, NATO's front line of defence against the enemy. I walked into my accommodation, jumped onto a bed, and immediately crashed out.

The next day we met the OC (officer commanding) – who welcomed us to the squadron – and the SSM (squadron sergeant major), who had the responsibility for disciplining us, identifying the 'do's and don'ts' relating to alcohol, bullying, and brothels. It soon became apparent that we'd have far more time on our hands than we'd had during basic training. I was assigned to 'F Troop' and allocated a brand new Bedford TM 4x4 vehicle. We then met our new troop commander, a first lieutenant straight out of Sandhurst, and then the troop staff sergeant, a very experienced soldier and expert in NBC (nuclear, biological, chemical) warfare.

The first few weeks were spent preparing for mobilisation, shooting on ranges, and undergoing first aid training and NBC familiarisation. The NBC threat was now real, and we soon found out that NBC training was the staff sergeant's favourite subject. As the squadron was on a tour of Northern Ireland, our role was to backfill, providing logistical support to the garrison and armoured division. We were instructed to be ready to mobilise at short notice – should orders to deploy be given – so we packed our personal equipment, ensuring we were ready.

The first mobilisation was called during the early hours one morning, so I got into combats, grabbed my personal equipment, and reported to stores to pick up the vehicle toolkit followed by the armoury to collect my rifle. After breakfast, we headed out in convoy fashion onto the open road, the role: to supply ammunition to front line artillery units, necessitating picking up armaments from depots and driving them four hours to the front line. This routine lasted for five days, and when not driving we'd be carrying out camp routine, the same skills we'd been taught back on Salisbury Plain sixteen months earlier.

The squadron returned back from Northern Ireland during late July, and they decided to spend the next few days getting tanked up and wanting to fight with everybody. Fortunately, this was short-lived, as everyone went home on leave, allowing all that unspent aggression to be expended by the time they returned.

On return from leave, I decided to volunteer for an exercise with the American Air Force. The brief was to drive to set locations, conceal ourselves, and try to avoid detection from *A-10 Warthog* aircraft. These were the real deal; heavily armoured tank killers capable of inflicting multiple damage. The aircraft would fly low over our heads, simulating real attacks using smoke and flares – a good choice, as the section was made up mostly from lads who'd just returned from Northern Ireland. We moved away from normal camp routine, deciding to make a camp out of straw bales, which actually resembled a house. Sentry duties were also dropped, allowing us to make full use of the local pub. I was now living the dream, in a house made of straw, making strong allies with the experienced soldiers from the squadron.

The exercise was followed by a week guarding a nuclear location in an undisclosed area, a rotating task carried out by troops serving in Germany. We were split into three sections: the first patrolled individually around the boundary wall, fully armed with live ammunition between watch towers. The QRF (quick reaction force) were on immediate standby – again fully armed should the location come under attack – with the backup section poised and ready to support the QRF. We never actually discovered what it was we were protecting, although rumours suggested that the actual nuclear arsenal was concealed elsewhere. This was the Cold War, a game of poker with double bluff being played out by both sides, making anything possible.

The next month was spent preparing for Exercise Lionheart, still recognised today as the largest deployment of NATO troops since the Second World War. We were going to be deployed for up to six weeks in the field, the exercise involving 130,000 British soldiers from both the regular and territorial army. The Royal Air Force (RAF) deployed over 13,000 personnel, including Harrier and Tornado squadrons. Opposition forces were made up from German, Dutch, American, and Commonwealth countries.

4 Armoured Division deployed over 24 hours, with my squadron being first to leave camp. The deployment with the American Air Force proved vital as my SC (section commander) had been on that exercise, meaning I had already established a good rapport. The section travelled south to the ammunition depots, picking up pallets loaded with artillery supplies before driving north to the first location, a large farm that would become our forward operating base for the foreseeable future. Déjà vu – my first exercise was being played out again. The squadron was based within the same vicinity comprising HQ (headquarters), the stores, the main field kitchen, and the fuel depot. We arrived early evening, reversed the vehicles into location, then draped hessian and camouflage netting over them before getting sent straight out on sentry duty.

The first five days saw no movement at all, and when not on sentry duty we sat around, relaxing and swapping stories of basic training, home life, and the NI tour. This allowed friendships to be forged and trust to be harnessed. I had witnessed so much in such a short time – junior leaders, trade training, and now the largest mobilisation of British troops ever seen. I was full of confidence, my mindset strong, even though I knew this wasn't going to be easy and that it was likely to get tougher as time went on.

When we were called to HQ to receive our orders, we were told to be ready to deploy, our role: to supply the forward artillery positions. With the briefing over, we went back to carry out our final checks. The call came during the early hours. We had removed the scrim netting at last light, leaving only the window hessian to be removed, and we departed location in convoy light until we picked up the main road. This phase was spent driving for many hours, picking up supplies from railway depots, and moving pallets to locations on the northern plains, where artillery units had established their tactical positions. This routine went on for days until we moved on to a new location.

After a day's rest, I was ordered to go on a specific detail to pick up medical supplies with another troop member. I had familiarised myself with the MSR (main supply route), and felt confident about heading out. We were driving through a small town when I noticed a group of what appeared to be students shouting and waving banners at the side of the road. We stopped at some traffic lights when they turned red, and as soon as the vehicle was stationary a few people ran over and lay down in the road directly in front of us. They then proceeded to climb up onto my cab, draping large 'Greenpeace' flags over the windscreen as they persistently tried to gain entry. After failing to gain entry, the protesters painted CND and peace logos all over the vehicle. We had two rifles with ammunition, and as we couldn't allow these to be taken, we were stuck there. The protest lasted twenty minutes, when the German police arrived to disperse the group. We were told to remain inside whilst the road was cleared, giving us a hasty exit. I drove back to location to be met by the SSM showing no sympathy, although I was convinced he secretly found it amusing. We were told to report to the stores to pick up green paint for the vehicle, but with no brushes to be found we had to settle for pastry brushes from the field kitchen. Needless to say, it was going to be a long night.

During this period, one of our troop members had been moved into a different section and was replaced with a 'ten week wonder', just out of basic training. He'd been catapulted straight onto exercise, and I couldn't help but feel sorry for him; he looked so lost.

"Hello, how's it going?" I asked him.

"Fine, thanks," he replied.

"Talk about being dropped in at the deep end! Let me give you a hand."

With that, I gave him a quick induction to life on exercise and what to expect over the coming weeks.

The next five weeks proved tough, driving long distances over many hours and delivering munitions to units all over the exercise area. The weather remained good, however, making living conditions favourable.

My lasting memory of Lionheart was when ENDEX (end of exercise) was called. It took seven days to return to camp, having to return all the supplies back to ammunition depots and getting caught up in long convoys – one reportedly over 30 miles long.

The next few weeks remained busy, before I went home for December. Then, after a quiet January, I got deployed on exercise Frozen Solid in mid-February, where temperatures got down to as low as minus 20 degrees, meaning we had to learn how to live in harsh artic conditions. I remember being incredibly cold the entire time; it was so cold the diesel actually froze. During this time we were trained to fight and survive in cold and wet conditions, the German winter providing the perfect environment.

I was soon made aware that the squadron were seeking volunteers to go to the Falklands for a four-month tour. This appealed to me; having watched all the events unfold at school, I desperately wanted to serve in the South Atlantic. At the same time, I was put forward for selection for an expedition – a double crossing of the Sahara Desert. It was being led by my troop commander, which would hopefully give me some home advantage.

I was interviewed for the Falklands, and attended the selection event for the expedition comprising fitness testing, command tasks, and yet more interviews. I was full of confidence, thinking I'd done well enough to secure a place, which I had. I was offered one of the positions – being tasked as cook – and as I only had a very limited knowledge of food preparation, I knew I'd have to learn fast. The only thing I had in common with cooking was my surname.

On my return from the desert, I travelled to Nijmegen in the Netherlands to participate in the four-day marches, the largest multiple-day marching event in the world. We participated in the military category, which required us to walk in 'fighting order', 40km per day, over four days. This was great fun, with the early mornings, walking until early afternoon, and then resting up until the next day. We were marching against military personnel from all over the world, giving us the opportunity to swap military clothing – we quickly learnt that the US Marine Corps desperately wanted British combat uniforms.

The biggest event of the summer followed, Live Aid, which we watched in the squadron bar over a really warm July weekend. The concert had been organised by pop artists Bob Geldof and Midge Ure in response to the famine in Ethiopia. The main memories I have of that day were watching Queen's frontman Freddie Mercury steal the show, and then Phil Collins playing *Against All Odds* and *In the Air Tonight* at Wembley Stadium – this was right before he travelled by Concorde to Philadelphia where he sung the two hits again, the same day on two different continents. Live Aid was reportedly watched by a television audience exceeding 1.9 billion – 40% of the world's population – and they raised $127 million for famine relief. I was left wondering how much money would make its way to the refugee camp I'd witnessed in the southern Sahara some two months earlier.

On return from summer leave, I received my posting to the British Military Hospital (BMH), Port Stanley, Falkland Islands. My ambition to go to the Falklands had now been realised.

11

SHIT, WE'RE GOING TO ROLL

After months of negotiation, and after the political clearance had been received, the double crossing of the Sahara Desert was finally approved, and my departure date was agreed. Permission was denied, however, for entry into Nigeria, cutting off the southern 400km loop to Kano. Fortunately, this didn't dampen spirits too much as the journey would still exceed 10,000km, 80% of which was identified as being on rough terrain. The aim was to be adventurous, with the journey containing elements of physical endurance, as well as being educational.

The team leader had undertaken some initial research, realising that the majority of the route was unmade piste, and that in some places there were no roads at all. The choice of vehicle, therefore, was critical, particularly for a return journey. The vehicle chosen was the ¾ ton Land Rover, proven by the army as being ideal for desert terrain. The first task was to paint the Land Rovers white and register them with civilian number plates, as all links to the military had to be removed.

Finally, the two vehicles set off from Minden on the 26-hour trip to Marseille. We camped overnight, having a cold beer and enjoying the calm before the storm. The 22-hour ferry journey was dreadful, made worse by rough seas and being surrounded by a kind of squalor I'd never seen before. We were met in Algiers by the Assistant Defence Attaché from the British Embassy, who navigated us through the customs formalities before driving with us to his residence, where we spent the evening. The following day we were introduced to our Algerian guide, who became the ninth member of the team.

With the formalities done, we headed off towards the Sahara, aiming for the French Foreign Legion fort of Laghouat, some 470km south of Algiers. We stopped for our first night in the desert and I got straight to work cooking the evening meal, using petrol burners to heat the pre-packed rations. Thankfully the meals were well received, confirming that my cooking methods were acceptable. The temperature soon dropped below freezing, so sunrise – at around 5.30 a.m. – was a welcome sight. We woke up, washed and shaved, and then I prepared jam sandwiches for breakfast. This was going to be our daily routine: get up early, have breakfast, leave early, drive all day until sundown, eat, and then go straight to bed. After 10 hours – and a further 400km – we'd reached El Golea, standing over 1100km away from the desert capital of Tamanrasset. The roads had now deteriorated to washboard piste, threatening to shake everything apart.

We awoke and pushed on for another 400km on the same road conditions until we reached the town of In Salah, marking the end of any proper road surface for the next 500km. This place was a squalid collection of mud bricked houses, with just one hotel and a garage. This came as a real shock to me, as it had been denoted as a major town on the map. While I was there I watched a camel being slaughtered, observing two men as they sliced the animal's throat, cut it up into small pieces, and placed the body parts into a makeshift trolley, something definitely not to be observed by the squeamish.

After spending the night in the small town, we pushed on through the emptiness of the desert for the next 650km, towards Tamanrasset. After driving for over 13 hours in temperatures reaching 39 degrees, we collapsed into our sleeping bags, totally shattered.

We left early the next day, reaching Arak mid-morning, although we chose not to stop there. 100km out of Arak, the road suddenly changed into a flat, open, rocky plain, allowing us to speed across the terrain.

Smash!

A large rock was thrown up by the lead vehicle, smashing our windscreen and forcing us to stop. The team mechanic carried out the repair, whilst we took a break in the 40+ degree midday sun. Once the problem was sorted, we continued south for the 250km journey to Tamanrasset, arriving late at night.

We had now been travelling for four days and had covered 2000km. We were all exhausted, the pungent smell of our body odour obvious. We enjoyed our first day out of the vehicle, therefore, taking showers and drinking cool Coca-Cola from the air-conditioned bar at the Hotel Tahat, a much-needed respite. We explored the town – a thriving centre of commerce right in the middle of the Sahara Desert – and I also got to observe the fierce and impressive Tuareg tribesmen, who had ruled this part of the Sahara since the start of the century.

I managed to purchase some local bread, plus some fruit, giving us a much-needed break from the jam sandwiches. We were waiting for word to depart south when one of the team noticed a snapped rear suspension unit: bad news, as it wasn't typically a spare item we carried. Our guide proved really useful, however – understanding the language and local customs – and a new spring was located and fitted, although the delay put us back 24 hours. During this time, two members of the team became very ill, suffering from high temperatures, headaches, and vomiting – classic symptoms of heatstroke. It was agreed that the two men would remain in Tamanrasset with the guide to recuperate.

The remaining six team members continued south for the Niger border as temperatures rose to the mid-40s. It took a full 24 hours to cover the 400km and to reach In Guezzam, the border post between Algeria and Niger. We had a frustrating three-hour wait at the border whilst Algerian officials tried to extort money out of the team leader, but he flatly refused – it was only when a local army commander intervened that we were allowed to travel the 50km to Assamaka, Niger's customs post.

Once through the customs post, we pushed on for Arlit, knowing it was a whole day away. This proved challenging due to the driving conditions – open desert with tracks heading in all directions –the only way through being to trust the compass and stick to the bearing.

We spent an entire day clearing Arlit police and customs, having to explain our presence in Niger; we got the feeling we were being interrogated, with the customs officers getting more and more agitated. Due to the developing situation, and satisfied that we'd reached tarmac on the southern edge of the Sahara, the team leader decided it was time to turn around and head back. The police then decided to escort both vehicles back to Assamaka by a different route, resulting in the vehicles getting stuck in thick patches of soft sand and having to self-rescue. After a five-hour wait in temperatures reaching 52 degrees, our passports were finally stamped and we were off again, travelling north back to In Guezzam.

There we were given a royal welcome by an Algerian army representative, who also gave us a super meal of fresh goat, ice-cold water, and the first proper beds we'd slept in for over two weeks. Suitably refreshed, the next morning the vehicles were refuelled for the journey back to Tamanrasset.

Travelling north and leaving In Guezzam behind us, we were witness to what surely must be one of the saddest sights the Sahara had to offer its travellers – a refugee camp. There were hundreds of refugees walking around in the desert sun, reportedly from neighbouring Niger. I remembered watching Michael Buerk's broadcast, reporting on the famine in Ethiopia, and his famous words, referring to what he saw as *"a biblical famine in the 20th century"* and *"the closest thing to hell on Earth"*.

By now we were used to the cross-country driving, making good time, and it turned into a bit of a race – before we realised anything was up, the two vehicles got separated. The piste was often 20 miles wide and very unclear, the correct path being marked at only 100km intervals by large empty oil drums. We had no contact with the other vehicle; we just hoped they'd continued north by accurate means of navigation.

We arrived back in Tamanrasset after completing 440km in seven hours – the best run yet on such ground – shortly followed by the other vehicle, a welcome sight for both teams. The next day was spent checking vehicles, repacking, and catching up on some much-needed rest. Both members who'd remained behind had now fully recovered and were looking forward to the return leg.

We pushed on and made good time to Arak, before travelling a further eight hours over the rough tracks back to In Salah. There, we took local advice about the next stage of the journey to Reggane, which wasn't good. We were advised that the route was fraught with difficulties and best avoided, the alternative being a two-day detour. After a brief debate, we agreed to go for it anyway.

Unfortunately, after about an hour into the journey, disaster struck. The vehicle I was travelling in hit a large rock, causing the tyre to blow out, the driver to lose control, and the vehicle to start rolling.

"Shit, we're going to roll!" I shouted out.

I watched the team leader surge forward in the front passenger seat and almost fly out of the broken windscreen before gravity pulled him back into his seat as the vehicle flipped over onto its roof.

"Get the fuck out!" someone shouted.

The fuel contained in the crushed roof rack started leaking onto us, soon followed by engine oil. Fortunately, the fuel didn't ignite and the four of us managed to escape unharmed.

"Fuck, that was close!" the team leader stated.

We climbed out of the windows with just minor injuries, and all we could do was look at one another and laugh – though the team leader didn't see the funny side.

Having winched the vehicle upright, the mechanic then checked it over and we nursed it back to In Salah, laughing all the way! The team leader still didn't share our sense of humour as he'd be the one facing the brigadier on our return, and would have to explain the damage sustained to one of the loaned vehicles. With that the 300km journey to Reggane was aborted, and we decided to camp just outside In Salah instead. After sunrise the next morning, we headed towards El Golea, some 400km north. The damaged vehicle performed perfectly, apart from the fact that the roof was now some 18 inches lower. The accident had left the Algerian guide quiet, but the team's morale was never higher, despite the sustained cuts and bruises.

After 3800km of rough terrain, we were now back on tarmacked roads. We camped outside Algiers, waiting for clearance to enter the city, and after two days we arrived back in Algiers, spending a further three days in the Defence Attaché's residence and swimming off the coast. The ferry left Algiers early June for the 24-hour return trip back to Marseille. We covered the 1500km back to Minden in just under 20 hours, with us driving non-stop except to refuel.

This was a once-in-a-lifetime opportunity, and it was certainly testing and educational. It showed me a lifestyle and land that most people never get to experience in their entire lives. I left the Sahara with a good understanding of and respect for desert life – and the dangers its vastness poses. This really tested me; failure had been staring us in the face for most of the trip, but maintaining a positive mindset allowed me to remain resilient, and my fitness levels ensured I was able to cope with the extreme conditions the desert decided to throw at me.

12

DESIRE THE RIGHT

I Left Germany and headed straight home for a period of leave, before travelling to Brize Norton for my onward journey to the Falkland Islands courtesy of British Airways.

We were a good hour into the flight, however, when the captain announced, "We are returning back to the UK, due to technical issues". We were asked to return to our seats whilst the cabin crew walked through the aisles, pulling down window blinds. This was worrying – particularly as it was a military flight – but it was made even worse when, on the final approach, I sneaked a look under the blind to see emergency vehicles waiting for us with their blue lights flashing. Thankfully we landed OK and exited quickly, leaving all our hand luggage on board. Afterwards we were told that British Airways had "received a credible bomb threat". After a short wait we were transported to some overnight accommodation whilst the aircraft was checked over. Finally we departed the following day, landing in Ascension Island eight hours later where we got to enjoy a stopover before the final part of the journey. I did, however, wish we had more than a fleeting two-hour visit; Ascension looked like a fantastic place to visit and warranted much more time than that. When we were 20 minutes from Mount Pleasant Airport (MPA), the aircraft was joined either side by two Phantom fighter jets for the remainder of the flight. The Falklands had first been sighted by English sea captain John Davies from his vessel 'Desire' in 1592, and now – 393 years later – I had sight of the same islands.

Upon landing we were transported to Port Stanley, arriving at the transition area an hour later. I was met there by a Scottish lad who told me to grab my bags for the short journey to the accommodation, and before long I'd arrived at my new home: a floating hotel docked on the shoreline opposite the British Military Hospital (BMH).

The following day I met the Company Sergeant Major (CSM), who explained my new role to me. This necessitated working 48 hours as an ambulance driver, followed by 24 hours as a duty driver, which required transporting hospital staff, picking up essential supplies, and conveying telecommunications. This would be a rolling rota working three days on, one day off, and it required me to live in the hospital when on duty. There were four of us from the RCT, with the remaining personnel from the Royal Army Medical Corps (RAMC) made up of combat medics, doctors, and surgeons. Nurses were recruited from Queen Alexandra's Royal Army Nursing Corps (QARANC).

Following a tour of the hospital I was handed a set of vehicle keys, later learning it was a Mercedes CV (captured vehicle) that had been seized from the Argentine Army. It was alleged that Mercedes had been left unpaid for this whole vehicle fleet, which was purchased solely for the invasion. He showed me the workings of the vehicle before telling me to explore the local area, pointing me in the direction of Port Stanley. I couldn't believe it; having watched the Falklands War from start to finish at the age of fifteen, I was now within touching distance of the famous port. In fact, I remember screaming with excitement as I headed out onto the gravel road. The coastline and mountains in the distance really were an amazing sight, with Stanley to the foreground. I passed a floating dock with a submarine in port, then arrived at the 'Welcome to Stanley' sign. I was here, and as I entered Port Stanley, all the film footage and photographs I'd seen over the last three years suddenly flashed before my eyes.

I drove down Philomel Hill, a steep descent onto the main road into Stanley, and passed the Globe Hotel before turning left down the main drag, which opened up to the most amazing views of the harbour. Next I passed the red post box outside the post office, before seeing an array of Union Jack flags flying high over many houses, emphasising that this was very much a British dependent sovereignty. I then passed the iconic Government House, where I had watched the Royal Marines hoist the Union Jack flag back in 1982.

I parked up and walked to the Liberation Memorial, later learning that it had been funded entirely by the islanders to commemorate the British and the support units that had served in the war.

IN MEMORY OF

ALL THOSE

THAT LIBERATED US

14 JUNE 1982

I took time to reflect on the war, and in particular the military personnel who had left Portsmouth Harbour on that sunny day back in April 1982 and had never returned home.

I then drove down an unmade track towards the end of town, soon coming across Moody Brook, the barracks where the small detachment of Royal Marines were based at the time of the invasion. From the barracks I could see the mountains in the distance, where the advancing British troops endured fierce battles as they made the final assault. After driving as far as I could, I turned around to head back whilst following a Sea King helicopter flying low over the harbour. As I approached the hospital, I remember watching a Phantom fighter jet making the final approach into RAF Stanley – wow. What a brilliant first day.

My first serious blue light job came on a Sunday afternoon; I was sitting in the hospital ward talking to a nurse when the pager went off, and after running to reception to meet the combat medic he told me there had been a serious accident on Surf Bay, a local beauty spot located on the far eastern tip of the island. As we approached the beach I could see a Land Rover on its roof with several people standing around it – something that made me smirk, having experienced the same fate a few months earlier. I was a little cautious with driving onto the beach for fear of getting stuck in the soft sand, but we had to get close; the situation didn't look good.

On arrival I was met by a small number of hostile locals; it was clear they weren't too keen on us being there. This came as a bit of a surprise as the military had an excellent relationship with the islanders, but I soon realised why we weren't welcome: the occupants were drunk and no doubt wanted to make a quick exit. The Falkland Islands Police Force – a welcome sight for us, at least – arrived just as the group were starting to get rowdy. The medic proceeded to check over the casualties whilst I spoke to a couple of girls, my first real interaction with the local population. It was clear they liked men in uniform, so much so that I even arranged to meet one of them later on at Victory Green, a local meeting point. Once we were ready, we transported the casualties back to hospital with the police in tow.

I met the girl on Victory Green – on the water's edge, overlooking the harbour – on a sunny day with a strong sea breeze, a typical spring day in that part of the world. We sat on the grass talking about our home lives, and she told me she lived on West Falkland and was schooling in Stanley. Suddenly, alarm bells went off in my head. I'd taken it on face value that she was over 16 – she certainly looked and acted like it – but clearly that wasn't the case. I stayed for another hour, finding out about life on the islands and her own experiences of the war, and then I left.

My role as duty driver was busy, collecting nurses from their accommodation and bringing them back to the BMH, waiting around whilst they undertook their handover meeting, and then taking the night shift home. On the way back I would pick up fresh supplies from the bakery and deliver them to the chef, who would always have my breakfast waiting for me – a fresh omelette. I would then make multiple trips into Stanley, delivering and receiving daily dispatches from the communication centre located at the end of town. I would also be on standby to take doctors on home visits, allowing time with the community. You were never alone whilst driving, as hitchhiking was prevalent and the expectation was to pick up service personnel between the accommodation and the town. Another, unofficial role was driving nurses to various locations, a role that later came to benefit me in terms of the connections I got to make.

A few days later, I was on Victory Green again when I was approached by a couple of locals. They demanded to know what my interest was in the girl I had met, basically warning me off – the girl had obviously told them about the time we'd spent together. I stood my ground, trying not to be concerned by their comments, but one woman was really hostile and left a lasting impression on me. It was clear that this was a close community, where everyone knew one another's business and where everyone watched each other's backs.

I really enjoyed making the most of my days off, as there was so much to see and do. I would always start with a run, taking in the coastal sites, mostly in windy conditions. Then, after a shower, I would walk into Stanley or go for a walk on nature trails, such as penguin walk or Surf Bay, wildlife watching. We also had access to off-road motorbikes, giving us the chance to see all the areas around Stanley, which were just waiting to be explored. The other activity I spent a lot of time on was flying with the RAF, courtesy of connections made through the nurses. The RAF were stationed at Stanley Airfield, where fighter jets, Sea King helicopters, and the Hercules squadron were all based. After the war, the airfield had been quickly established as the main station for the RAF due to its close proximity to Stanley.

After the invasion, the Argentinians did nothing to extend or improve the runway, apart from adding anti-aircraft weaponry. During the conflict, the runway gave a major strategic advantage to the Argentine Air Force, allowing transport planes and combat aircraft to operate. The British response was the planning and execution of 'Operation Black Buck', a series of long-range missions from Ascension Island where the key objective was to attack the airfield and associated defences. This necessitated air-to-air refuelling between a number of tankers and two Vulcan bombers. The raids were successful, with a single crater being made on the runway, rendering it impossible for fast jets to attack the British task force. The mission is still regarded as one of the longest-ranged bombing raids in history.

My first trip of the *1312 Flight* was on board the C-130 Lockheed Hercules, a four-engine turboprop transport aircraft. This was an astonishing flight, flying out over West Falkland and being tracked by two phantom jets – their mission to locate our position and missile lock their weapon systems onto our aircraft. To avoid this, the pilot would have to dive into steep descents – the manoeuvrability of these aircraft was unreal. Other trips included air-to-air refuelling, watching the phantoms being refuelled through a small hole towards the back of the plane – being that close, you could actually see the whites of the pilot's eyes. The maritime patrols would last much longer; this involved checking up on foreign fishing vessels in the waters around the islands and ensuring they held the relevant licences, as those waters were lucrative.

The blue light jobs remained relentless, carrying military and civilian casualties from across Stanley, with the helicopter landing pad next to the hospital having to be used when casualties were flown from camp settlements or surrounding waters. When picking up from the helipad I would reverse up, swing open the back doors, and await the arrival of the casualties. This was a swift operation, particularly with the Chinooks, with the strong downwinds from the rotating blades creating a vast downdraught and making conditions difficult.

I was sitting in reception when a call came in confirming a Chinook was inbound from MPA with a cardiac arrest on board. A senior naval officer had stepped off the inbound flight from the UK and had fallen over as he stepped onto the tarmac, going into cardiac arrest. He was placed on the floor whilst the surgeon took charge, and I was involved with the entire incident, from watching the Chinook land through to the surgeon stopping cardiopulmonary resuscitation (CPR) after approximately 40 minutes or so. It struck me how this man had come all this way but hadn't got to witness the beauty of the Falklands – and how he'd be returning to the UK in the cargo hold.

A few days before Christmas I was sitting in the reception area when I heard shouting and screaming coming from outside. I jumped up and ran out to find the woman I'd had words with arguing with a male soldier. I separated the pair, sent the soldier away, and brought her inside. It became clear that she'd been having words over him seeing a local girl. The medic checked her over before discharging her, and with that she was gone. I had seen her around town, but we never spoke due to the hostility she'd shown me early on. This encounter made me even more interested, and for some reason I felt attracted to her. I wanted to get to know her, even though it was madness – after all, she'd warned me off previously, and had been admitted to hospital for the same reason. Plus, she was an islander, so I thought there was no chance of anything happening.

I worked through Christmas, which was a busy time spent dealing with lots of drunken people requiring minor treatments. Then, for NYE, I went to a fancy dress party at a bar up at the female accommodation area, dressed as a surgeon. The bar was busy, with everyone enjoying the evening, and there was plenty of drinking and cavorting going on. I spent the early part of the evening with some nurses before realising the local woman was in the same room; I hadn't recognised her initially due to her fancy dress outfit. Eventually our eyes met and she walked over, and although I was thinking 'here we go again', she just commented on my appearance before making a suggestive comment. I spoke to her for a while, and then she told me she'd be back at midnight.

Midnight arrived, and sure enough I was joined by the woman, who threw her arms around my neck and pulled me close until our mouths met. We stayed embraced for what seemed like ages, before she pulled back and asked me to walk her home. I couldn't believe it; I was totally confused, thinking she didn't like the military. When the party ended, I sneaked out to meet up with her and to walk her home, holding hands the whole way. We were back at her house in no time, and she told me to stay downstairs so as not to wake her house mate. I was nervous, and rightly so considering I was still inexperienced when it came to sex. Besides, I didn't want to suffer the same fate I'd experienced with my first girlfriend.

She sat next to me on the sofa, moving ever closer until we were touching, and then we turned and started kissing passionately. Wow, it felt nice, all that hostility gone in an instant. She was wearing a dress with buttons running up the front, and she allowed me to touch her body. We were both drunk, our inhibitions gone, and before I knew it I felt her hand pressing hard against my belt buckle – new territory for me. I left her hand there whilst I started touching her breasts, then she whispered in my ear that we needed to move for fear of getting caught, so I followed her into the downstairs bathroom, locking the door behind me. I lay on the floor and she sat on top of me, pushing herself hard against my body. It wasn't long before she'd removed my trousers and her underwear and we were having sex, something that went on until the early hours. I kissed her goodbye before walking back home, where I showered and reported for work –fortunately on ambulance duty, as I was worn out. It was a good way to start the year.

I continued to see the woman, staying in her house on my days off – and fortunately moving from the bathroom into her bedroom. I had quickly transformed from being a rabbit caught in the headlights to having a lot more confidence in the bedroom, thanks to my encounters on this tour. The only downside was that I'd allowed feelings to creep into the relationship, and the timing wasn't particularly good as I was starting to prepare to leave these islands, having received my new posting: a tour to Belize in Central America. My last week was emotional, as I'd fallen in love both with this place and with an islander, but even so it was time for me to leave. My time in the South Atlantic was coming to an end.

13

STIMS TO HOLDFAST

Déjà vu – I was en route to Brize Norton for my journey to Belize, this time on board a VC10, courtesy of the RAF. We flew there via Gander in Northern Canada – where the snow on the ground was towering over three metres high – and we landed in Belize adjacent to Airport Camp, my new home for the next six months. The first thing that hit me as I walked down the steps was the intensity of the heat; it was a similar sensation to opening an oven door, and was a million miles from the weather I'd experienced a few hours earlier in Gander.

We were met by the troop sergeant who took the new arrivals to the accommodation: a prefabricated steel-structured 'Nissen hut' comprising 24 beds, each one protected by a mosquito net. We were given five minutes to find an empty bed space prior to taking the camp tour, then we walked down to the guardroom (located next to the camp hospital), followed by the NAAFI, the swimming pool, and finally, the bar. Next we were taken to stores, where we were issued with jungle combats, shorts, bush hats, and waterproofs – our clothing requirements for the tour. We were then told to report to the guardroom at 05.00 for the weekly fitness test, known as the 'yellow brick road run'.

Waking up was easy, with the temperature rapidly rising and the sunlight starting to shine in through the windows. The squadron was formed up outside the guardroom, and then we headed out on the 3km run, a circular route on a yellow dusty surface. I was in my element again, staying with the leading pack before heading back for a cold shower. I was also really chuffed to meet two Gloucester Troop lads halfway through their tours. Back at the room, I was greeted by a Belizean lady who offered her services to clean my bed space and do my laundry for $10 a week – a bargain, especially as it soon became apparent that our clothing needed washing daily.

The first month was difficult, having to adjust to jungle life, the early mornings, the hot humid weather, and the darkness falling early. Having a strong mindset and a healthy immune system was important due to the nasty diseases you could pick up out there. I spent the first month constantly being bitten by mosquitos and sand flies, which would leave you constantly scratching. The only safe haven was under the shower, as it was free from humidity and parasites, particularly mosquitos. Although the shower protected you from parasites, however, it didn't protect you from Belizean Blue Crabs, a large crab – large enough to attack you – the size of a football with a huge left snapping claw.

This was a fully operational tour, meaning we had duties every day. When I got there I was given a two-hour tour of Belize City, where I was taught to drive around the city in the wrong direction, purposely against the one-way system – although it was never explained why. This practice made the Belizeans angry, and rightly so! The first driving job allocated to new arrivals was the 'shit truck', which required going around camp with two Belizeans on board, tidying rubbish and emptying bins. The fun would start as you entered the landfill site, where out of the jungle canopy people would appear, jumping onto the back of the vehicle and sifting through the rubbish. By the time I'd reach the site, most of the items would have been removed; one man's rubbish was clearly another man's gold.

The next detail – the 'stims run' to Holdfast Camp – dragged on for two months. This involved driving a Land Rover and trailer across treacherous roads, crossing bridges and ravines at speed, and carrying fizzy drinks (referred to as stims) to the resident battle group – at the time, 40 Commando. At this point the marines were coming to the end of their tour, being replaced by 6/7 Queens Regiment.

I had gone from sharing a room with one person in the Falklands to now sleeping in a large open space accommodating 23 other men. I managed to secure a corner bed space, allowing some privacy, but more importantly it permitted the mosquito net to be suspended correctly, allowing 100% protection. The privacy was essential, but it didn't shield you against the snoring, farting, and occasional shouting out that were normal nightly occurrences. There was one lad who kept us awake every night due to his constant snoring; he was a Para, a gentle giant, who would get carried outside in his bed and then left there. You would always know when he'd woken up, as you'd hear him shouting, *"Who the fuck moved me again?"* This would always result in someone having to help him carry his bed back inside the room.

Belize City, located a few miles away, was a dangerous place for the military to be, and therefore it was forbidden to visit on your own. My first trip out was to the 'Rose Garden', a bar and brothel located within the same premises. The bar was rowdy, full of marines on their last week of tour, and we were having a drink when it suddenly kicked off, tables and chairs flying everywhere – time to leave. There was a well-built marine manning the front door, and as I walked towards him he grabbed my arm and shouted, *"Give me the fucking regimental corps motto!"*

"Per Mare, Per Terram!" I replied.

"Nice one, lads, out you go," came the reply.

He was obviously looking out for his boys, thinking we were marines, and providing safe passage. Thankfully my time in the cadets proved helpful, allowing us a quick exit, and we jumped into a taxi just as the Royal Military Police (RMP) started to arrive.

I also took part in the 'Run the World' event, where I ran 10km with my Scottish mate, both of us donning our branded t-shirts. The run was held simultaneously in 89 countries, timed to coincide with a UNICEF conference in New York City. I later found out that my brother had undertaken the run in Hyde Park, London at the same time, with members of my karate dojo.

Belize was superb for water-based activities, being surrounded by beautiful cayes (islands off the mainland) offering a range of activities including sailing, kayaking, and scuba diving. The army had their own base on St. Georges Caye, a water-based mecca allowing downtime to be well spent. Cayes boasted great beaches, palm trees, clear blue sea, and bundles of sunshine. Regular trips included Caye Caulker and San Pedro on the mainland; San Pedro, or 'La Isla Bonita' is now a tourist mecca and was made famous by Madonna's song of the same name. San Pedro was a great destination for two reasons: the mode of transport, which was always a Puma helicopter, allowing you to book the front seat next to the pilot, and the selling of contraband to the locals. We would buy cheap cases of 'Schlitz' beer on camp, stuff them into bags, and then sneak the merchandise to San Pedro to sell, creating a good profit margin in the process.

The other destination we spent a lot of time at was a little known place in Mexico called Cancun. Getting to Cancun was easy; it was a straightforward journey of turning left out of camp and heading north until you crossed the border at Quintana Roo, arriving at Cancun three hours later. Cancun was not well known in 1986, but it was recognised as the playground for young Americans. It was the perfect combination of great weather, white sandy beaches, all-inclusive resorts, and nightclubs that pulsated till sunrise. This was good news for military boys, especially as the American college girls loved our accents and were on vacation to have a good time.

Three months into my tour I was seconded to the camp hospital because of my previous experience. Like the BMH, it consisted of two roles: ambulance driver, requiring me to live in the hospital, and working with the Field Surgical Team (FST). The team comprised a surgeon, an anaesthetist, and two operating theatre technicians (OTT).

This was an imperative 'hearts and minds' role undertaken by the army; it was important to reach out to the local population, and this was done by making direct contact, building bridges, and gaining trust. I was responsible for preparing the Land Rover and trailer, and then driving to local towns and villages where the temporary theatre would be set up, including everything required for the day: the tent, surgical appliances, oxygen cylinders, anaesthetic, and routine drugs. The surgeon was an RAF officer, and the anaesthetist was a Falkland's veteran who'd worked at Ajax Bay Field Hospital during the conflict, saving both British and Argentinian soldiers' lives, often while under enemy fire. The two technicians were both sergeants from the RAMC.

On arrival, we set up the theatre in the tent or used the buildings provided, the list of routine operations having already been agreed, allowing the team to commence straight away. I would 'scrub up', then assist the anaesthetist with putting the patients to sleep before helping out in the recovery room. After surgery, we would all help pack up before driving to a roadside café for an enjoyable meal and an ice-cold drink. I was now in the company of senior ranking officers, carrying out an important role for the army and living the dream yet again.

Whilst living in hospital I got introduced to a new passion, the album 'Bat out of Hell' by Meat Loaf. I had never come across it before, as it was never a genre I was particularly into. A medic played it every evening during night shift, however, getting me hooked. I appreciated Ian Dury for his reference to real life, always telling stories through his lyrics, and Meat Loaf was no different – the album being a love story played out over time. I learnt all the tracks, likening some to my time spent in the Falklands.

During the tour, all military personnel received two weeks' holiday, during which you had the option of flying back to the UK or travelling to Florida or Mexico. The FIFA World Cup was being staged in Mexico, so I decided to opt for a two stay holiday, first in Acapulco and then in Cancun. It was an excellent two weeks, spending a week with a beautiful Mexican girl in Acapulco and then partying hard in Cancun while watching World Cup matches. The tournament was eventually won by Argentina, captained by Diego Maradona, who beat West Germany 3-2 in the final. Maradona scored the 'Hand of God' goal against Peter Shilton during the quarter-final match against England, a goal that remains as controversial today as it was back in 1986.

F Troop were living on camp, going about their daily business alongside the other units. They were easy to spot as they had their own dress code and they carried the M16 rifle, fitted with the 40mm grenade launcher under the barrel. One day I was sitting in the hospital talking to who I assumed was a doctor, and he told me he was a serving member of the SAS, medically trained and seconded to the hospital. He also told me that members of 23 SAS (Reserve) were visiting and had requested medical support for a training exercise on Mountain Pine Ridge. I jumped at the opportunity.

I had visited this area previously and knew it was the perfect training environment, with densely packed Honduras pine trees located in a mix of grasslands, granite, and limestone deposits with an array of topographical extremes – the highest point, Baldy Beacon, stood over 1,016m high, with the lowest point being the Macal River.

I got to spend a few days with the SAS, working closely with the small teams and getting a small insight into their world. They were dropped off by a Puma helicopter before going out on all-day patrols, gathering intelligence. I also got to ride in a Puma tasked with picking up F Troop patrol members from locations along the Guatemalan border. I watched the pilot land within small clearings in the jungle canopy, at which point the door would open and a heavily bearded soldier would jump in, carrying either a shotgun or an M16.

Towards the end of my time in Belize I received my new posting: I was going back to the Falklands. This was great news – I would be entering my third consecutive summer and going back to a place I loved.

14

ASCENSION 1815

Arriving back in England was a welcome relief. With the humidity gone, I was no longer hot and bothered; the jungle environment had certainly taken its toll on me. I'd lost weight, I had scars all over my body from parasite bites, and I'd returned home somewhat disheartened, feeling exhausted through a lack of proper sleep. It felt good to be in a room on my own again, without having to negotiate a mosquito net hanging over my bed space. Fortunately, I managed to snap out of my mood quickly. Both of my parents gave me some much-needed encouragement, and it also helped that I was now focusing on my return to the South Atlantic.

I spent the month catching up with family and friends, as well as meeting my future brother-in-law, who had started dating my sister. I also spent a lot of time with my younger brother playing golf, riding bikes, and messing around in the local park. My social life at home had now moved on loads thanks to my new-found confidence with women, as well as the two groups of friends I had to hang out with: my school friends and my mates from the dojo, who I'd remained in close contact with. Although the town was full of pubs, a new wine bar on the high street had quickly established itself as the place to be. Wednesdays and Fridays were '80's nights', playing hits from my school years and always within a great party atmosphere. While I was there one night I met a British Airways stewardess who was a few years older than me, and we had a brief relationship, even getting to spend a weekend in Guernsey together, courtesy of her flight concessions.

The month flew by, and it wasn't long before I was on the way back to Brize Norton. I didn't realise it at the time, but something was about to happen that I couldn't help but question. I was sitting in the departure lounge when I watched the woman from the Falklands casually walk in. I couldn't believe it – I'd last seen her in Port Stanley, and now here she was, flying on the same aircraft as me. I didn't speak to her initially, so I was left speculating as to what she'd been doing here in the UK. When we landed in Ascension Island, however, I finally broke the silence before we boarded again, and as the seat next to mine was empty, I invited her to join me, allowing me time to find out what she'd been up to over the last few months. As we started to see land appear, I remember looking out of the window and watching the Phantom fighter jets join our aircraft, signalling that we'd soon be landing.

It was easy settling in, having served on the islands only eight months earlier; nothing had changed, and my duties remained the same. I was back driving the same Mercedes CV, and the skies were still full of Sea Kings, Chinooks, and Phantom fighter jets. The accommodation and the hospital were exactly as I'd left them, with just one significant change: the hospital team. They were all new, as my friends from the previous tour had moved on to serve in new units around the world.

I met up with the woman a couple of times, but by then we'd both moved on. It was a good thing really, especially as I was starting to get attention from the nurses – and as I was now in a position to respond to their advances.

Halfway through the tour I boarded a UK-bound flight on board an RAF TriStar, this time jumping off at Ascension Island – something I'd wanted to do ever since stepping onto this island for the first time. I had now been gifted this privilege courtesy of my second tour. I was really excited; this island had so much history, and its location on the planet – sitting near the Equator in the South Atlantic Ocean – made it truly unique. The welcome sign stated that the island was part of the British Overseas Territory of Saint Helena, Ascension, and Tristan da Cunha.

The original settlement of Ascension began in 1815, when the British garrisoned it after imprisoning Napoleon on neighbouring Saint Helena. The island was then claimed for King George III due to its unique location. Charles Darwin even visited it in 1863, referring to it as a 'dry treeless island'. The islands were then used as a base during World War Two, and as the staging post for the Falklands War. The runway was extended and widened, allowing it to be used for American bombers during the Cold War, and later as the emergency runway for the Space Shuttle. The RAF also conducted Operation Black Buck from there.

We stayed in the capital, Georgetown – which comprised a post office, a police station, and a small supermarket – and we spent most of our time on the American Air Force base drinking Budweiser beers and eating steak burgers. The weather was pleasant, with sunny days and temperatures reaching the 30s. I felt privileged spending time there, especially considering it was a destination strictly forbidden to tourists.

On my return to the Falklands I joined a battlefield tour of Mount Longdon, where 3 Para had captured the mountain over the 11th/12th June 1982.

The Argentine Army had gained advantage by constructing strong defensive positions high on the mountainside, but it was critical for 3 Para to capture the mountain if they were to advance onto Port Stanley. 3 Para had tabbed (Tactical Advance to Battle) from San Carlos Bay to establish a base near Murrell Bridge, located just over a mile away from the slopes of Mount Longdon.

The attack, which commenced on the 11th June, was ordered to be a silent one. As the Paras advanced, however, an anti-personnel mine went off, immediately giving away their position. The ferocious battle that followed lasted over ten hours, with 3 Para being pinned down for long periods due to the effective firepower laid down by the high Argentine machine gun positions. During the battle Sergeant Ian MacKay led an attack, gaining success and allowing 3 Para to make their advance. Sgt Mackay was killed during the attack, and later awarded a posthumous Victoria Cross for his gallantry.

By the end of the battle, 3 Para had lost 23 men, with a further 43 being wounded. The Argentinean losses were recorded at between 30 and 50, with up to 120 wounded and a small number captured. When I went, I was sitting on top of Mount Longdon on a warm summer's day, four years after the battle, witnessing first-hand this harsh environment and imagining how unforgiving these conditions must have been on that night. All I could do was sit in silence whilst observing the many battle fragments still lying on the ground around my feet.

This concluded my time in the Falklands – another brilliant tour, seeing and doing so much within such a short time. I loved these islands for their beauty, their wildlife, and their sense of community. On that front I got to say goodbye to the woman, which I found hard, as the time we'd spent together was very special – after all, she was the one who'd taken my virginity!

I had made lots of friends, visited Ascension Island, and was now looking forward to a period of leave before joining 66 Squadron, Tidworth.

15

REALISING THE DREAM

I arrived home in time to pick up the last remnants of winter – having escaped the last two by being in the southern hemisphere – and went straight to the wine bar to meet up with my friends and catch up on the news. My mantra whenever I returned home was "all the same faces in all the same places". Whilst I'd been working on the other side of the world, my friends' lives had remained pretty much the same – although my karate mates had been training hard and winning major titles. By now – thanks to the strict teaching methods from the Shihan – the karate club had established itself as one of the toughest dojos in the country, producing world-class fighters.

I arrived in Tidworth and immediately reported to the guardroom to be shown to my accommodation. These were dilapidated communal buildings, and I later learnt I would receive reduced rent due to the poor living conditions – something I took as a good compromise considering it resulted in more money in my pay packet. As the squadron were away skiing – meaning I had the whole camp to myself – I decided to throw myself into fitness by running around the hills of Salisbury Plain, all within eyeshot from my accommodation.

The squadron arrived back late on the Friday, then everyone promptly disappeared for the weekend; I was astonished that everyone had literally dumped their kit and were gone within minutes, leaving me alone again! I used the time to explore the garrison, soon realising that there was nothing going on in Tidworth – probably the reason everybody went home!

When Sunday night arrived the camp started filling up again, allowing me to mix with the lads from my room. I soon realised they were all 10-week wonders straight out of Aldershot, only a few weeks into their first unit, and I was surprised they'd been posted to a unit within spitting distance of where they'd completed their training just weeks earlier; I was left wondering why they hadn't been deployed to Germany where the Cold War was still in full swing.

I was interviewed by the OC, who welcomed me to the squadron and who used this opportunity to set out my immediate ambition. He was surprised that I hadn't gained promotion and that I only held a basic trade qualification; I had chosen to go on operational tours rather than chase promotion, though I now realised this had left me on the back foot. He told me to sign up immediately for the Junior Military Qualification Certificate (JMQC), saying that he'd put me forward for trade training and the PTI course. As I'd already passed the JMQC, I wouldn't have to endure the five weeks of bullshit, inspections, and relentless show parades.

I quickly settled into the squadron – its role being to support UK Land Forces – and after a couple of months I realised that serving in the UK was very different. It was an eight-to-four job and everybody went home at the weekends; it lacked the camaraderie I'd become accustomed to.

There were regular details to Aldershot as well as a number of tactical exercises that took place throughout the country, though there was also plenty of downtime, allowing boredom to slowly creep in. We were always getting ready for mobilisation, spending hours making preparations for deployment – a status that was coined 'hurry up and wait'. It was now 1987 but, less than three years later, all the hours spent preparing for mobilisation would actually come to fruition for 66 Squadron with a deployment to the Gulf. Saddam Hussein had invaded Kuwait in 1990, leading to Operation Desert Shield – where operations would lead to the build-up of British and coalition forces in the Gulf region in readiness for the combat phase known as Desert Storm.

As nothing was going on at camp I started going home at weekends, trying to establish a social life again; I'd drive up the A303 and around the M25, and I'd be in the wine bar by early evening. It was during these times that I kept bumping into a girl called Jayne who I took a liking to, but although we went out a couple of times it didn't go anywhere. So, I decided to start heading up to the clubs in London with some mates from the dojo – nights that entailed jumping around crowded dance floors drinking bottled water whilst being surrounded by people high on Ecstasy. I thought this was madness, as it wasn't something I'd witnessed before, but it was simply the scene back then. Personally, I would get drunk before entering the clubs; I never had the desire to take drugs, having been warned off them so many times by medics in Belize.

As promised, the OC put me forward for my trade training and PTI course – and I was accepted for both. Before long I'd commenced driver training, spending two weeks driving HGV trucks around the Wiltshire countryside in readiness for my test date. With the training completed, I then attended trade training based in Aldershot to enhance my skill set. I worked hard to attain the relevant passes, also receiving Best Student in the process. On my return I was deployed for a month supporting the Parachute Regiment, who were jumping throughout Scotland. This proved to be great fun, especially as I spent my days off walking in the mountains.

After Scotland I travelled home for a month, taking the time to get my fitness up as I knew I'd be going straight to Aldershot to commence my training as a PTI at the Army School of Physical Training on Course 185. I had spent time in the gym with the squadron PTIs, familiarising myself with training methods and learning the standards that were required to pass the course. It was clear, therefore, that it was going to be tough, with the emphasis on instructing recruit and trained soldiers in PT as well as undertaking assault courses, log runs, basic and combat fitness tests, gymnastics, basketball, and boxing.

Whilst on leave I went for a long run one evening with a friend who was training for the Royal Marines, and as we passed the wine bar, we looked at each other and decided to go in, cutting our run short. We met up with some mates, totally unplanned, and then two stunning girls walked in. I was immediately drawn to one of them; she was short, had a well-toned, muscular body, and had cropped platinum blonde hair. Basically, she looked like Madonna in the 'Papa Don't Preach' video. I made eye contact with her and she came across with her friend – who I later found out was her sister – who started speaking to my friend. We had a brilliant evening, and we all ended up at my friend's house for the night. They were both Australians on holiday, and they were lapping up all the attention; Australia was very much in vogue in 1987, especially with *Neighbours* and Kylie Minogue bursting onto the scene. That month was mostly spent in the wine bar, making last-minute preparations for my upcoming course and planning days out with my new girlfriend.

I turned up late one Sunday evening at Queen's Avenue, Aldershot, to start the course and was taken to the accommodation sited opposite the PT School. This was it: years earlier I had stepped into the gym at Colerne totally awestruck by the PTIs – and their crossed swords insignia they all wore. Now, all that stood between me and earning the right to wear that same insignia was seven weeks of hard work. Bring it on!

On the Monday morning we stood in line in lightweight trousers, boots, and combat jackets in readiness for the timed BFT. Once completed, we were taken to the pool to undertake the military swim test, cementing my right to remain on the course. We were then told that we would march between the accommodation and the school, but as soon as we entered the school the squad would have to break into 'double time' – necessitating running – as walking was strictly prohibited within the grounds of the school.

The first week was taken up with practising and being tested on a number of skills including gymnastics, rope climbing, and upper body exercises. The rest of the week was spent learning to teach recruit soldiers PT, with my time in karate and junior leaders proving vital. The course was made up of soldiers from regiments from all over the British Army – including the Gurkhas, who I hadn't worked with before, but who I soon realised were strong and loyal soldiers. The course was split into three different sections who would all be competing against one another for the coveted Intersection Flag. The Gurkhas were in my section – great, I thought.

The Gurkhas are great soldiers, and their plight truly amazing, having had to travel across from Nepal to attend the selection process for the British Army. For those who are successful it is regarded as a great honour that carries much kudos in Nepal. Years later, I would get to experience their culture during a trip to Everest Base Camp.

Over the next four weeks I got to spend many hours competing in BFTs and CFTs, log runs, and the assault course. For example, during a single session on the assault course I would have to scale the course over 20 times, taking it in turns as either instructor or class participant. By now I had passed the recruit PT syllabus and moved onto basketball, boxing, trampolining, advanced gymnastics, and trained soldiers' PT.

With being so close to home I still managed to go back at weekends – a welcome break that allowed me to spend quality time with my girlfriend. The course flew by, and it wasn't long before we were into test week, a week during which we also competed to be Champion Section to win the Intersection Flag. Adopting the same attitude I'd carried with me since childhood, I achieved a B Grade, along with an 'excellent' recommendation permitting me to return to the Army School of Physical Training to undertake the advanced course within 18 months. The icing on the cake was being in the winning section and being awarded the Intersection Flag.

I was in a really good place; I was now in a position to wear the crossed swords and one stripe, having been promoted to Lance Corporal, on my ceremonial dress at my sister's wedding – which was planned for the same weekend as I finished the course. I had prepared my uniform and bulled my boots in readiness to leave on the Friday morning, and I went to sleep as normal, but I remember being woken up during the night by a window being blown wide open following a massive gust of wind. Closing the window, I thought nothing more of it and went straight back to sleep.

When I woke up on the Friday morning it was to complete devastation: a violent hurricane had made its way across the UK, France, and the Channel Islands. There were power cuts, and forests, parks, railway lines, and roads were closed due to being strewn with fallen trees – but I had to get home. The army had also been put on standby to provide an emergency response, so I received permission to leave straight away, though it took me six hours to get home due to all the long diversions.

The event now referred to as the 'Great Storm of 1987' was cited as a 1-in-200-year storm, and it caused over two billion pounds' worth of damage. Most people can remember the storm, though it is perhaps remembered more for the comments made by the BBC weatherman Michael Fish, who suggested that a lady had contacted the BBC warning them of the hurricane, but he dismissed it as a false alarm – though he claims he was misquoted.

The wedding went ahead as planned, with the electricity being replaced by candles in the church and the route to the reception having to be cleared out by chainsaws. Despite the storm, the day turned out perfectly, and I felt so proud to attend the wedding – along with a soldier friend – wearing ceremonial dress, as well as showing off my PT School insignia whilst posing for photographs with the wedding party.

It was now heading towards Christmas, and although I'd tried to get into the squadron gym, I was told there were no vacancies – which was critical as I wanted to return to the PT school with the intention of joining the Corps. Around the same time I was told that as I hadn't passed my HGV test within six months of passing the trade training, I would therefore have to undertake the five-week course again – despite attaining Best Student. I objected to this but no one listened to me, and my request of becoming the squadron PTI was also blocked, so it was back to the vehicle park. I did get to undertake the squadron's physical training alongside other duties, but I needed to be full-time in the gymnasium. They say that things come in threes... well, the final blow was that the upcoming United Nations (UN) peacekeeping tour of Cyprus had been withdrawn from UK forces, the role instead being transferred to units in BAOR. Having received three major drawbacks in quick succession, I saw Christmas as a welcome break.

Spending time at home was great, although the Australian sisters headed back to Australia shortly after Christmas – yet another blow for me to deal with. My parents were away on holiday so I had no one to speak to, and I started properly contemplating my future in the army. I had finally realised my ambition of becoming a squadron PTI – I knew this was my vocation, and that I was good at it – but I was being blocked. I also had the prospect of having to undertake the trade training all over again and I wasn't even going to Cyprus now, something I'd thought would break the monotony of serving in the UK. It was like being back in junior leaders, poised with a double-edged sword dilemma. I had realised my dream and knew I was good at it, and although I wanted to take my career to the next level, I was being blocked all the same.

I didn't particularly enjoy serving in the UK, so Cyprus had been my motivation – but it was now no longer an option. So, I decided to return to the squadron with the view of becoming a full-time PTI; either that or apply for a discharge, as I didn't want to return to normal duties now that I was a qualified PTI. After various discussions with my troop commander, it was clear that the year was going to be quiet and that I wouldn't be able to get into the gym to advance my chosen career for at least 18 months. After many hours of soul-searching, I decided to PVR (Premature Voluntary Release) from the army. I simply couldn't remain in Tidworth any longer.

At my exit interview, the OC asked me what I was going to do, so I told him I wanted to travel as this was the only thing I really knew. I was discharged a month later. My lasting memory is of going to the unit stores and handing back my clothing and equipment that had been issued to me at Colerne, although I still had to retain an essential set to fulfil my role as a reservist soldier. In an instant, my army career was over and I was driving back to Sussex, not knowing what would be waiting for me.

A few weeks later I was at home, contemplating my next move, when the phone rang. I couldn't believe it: it was the Australian woman, the one I'd been seeing. She was sitting on Manly Beach, telling me that she missed me and that she wanted me to go to Australia to spend time with her in Sydney! Well, there was no debate to be had: I was gone.

The army truly did define me, absolutely making me into the person I became. Once you leave the military you're on your own, having to enter this new world referred to as 'Civilian Street'. After all, when you're in the military it does everything for you: you're told when to go to bed, when to get up, when to eat, when to stand still, turn left, turn right, halt... orders, orders, orders. Absolutely everything is mapped out for you, whilst being backed up by the best military training establishment in the world, ensuring you can always do your job well when called upon to do so. You are then thrown into this new life where nobody really cares at all and where people aren't at all interested in you or your background. I'd been used to working in an environment of teamwork, where strong bonds were forged, and where loyalty and trust stood for everything, and now... all that was gone.

Despite being a wayward child, discipline had featured heavily in my childhood whilst I was at home, both at primary school and through sport. Judo and karate were both vital in laying the foundations for me, setting me up perfectly for junior leader training. The strict practices employed by my Shihan gave me the confidence and the personal resilience required to make it through the hard basic training regime. I had left home at sixteen, which – by anyone's reckoning – is considered young. You're still finding out about the world and still immature on all counts, so when I was thrown into the alien world of reward and punishment I was initially traumatised, citing it as my Baptism of Fire.

I knew that the foundations I set throughout childhood – and that I carried on through sport and the experiences I gained during my army career – would give me the best possible chance of success as I entered the next chapter of my life. By now I was well acquainted with failure, and as I'd met my personal ambitions I could now start to focus on setting new ones. More importantly, I now understood my own mindset, and I continued to retain exercise as my number one priority.

16

A ROOM WITH A VIEW

Whilst at middle school, I remember studying Australia in geography, learning that there was little known about this place – other than that it was considered to be upside down, that it was located on the other side of the world, and that the sea that surrounded it was full of great white sharks. We also learnt that this country was part of the Commonwealth – with strong ties to Great Britain and with the Queen as their Head of State – and that Aboriginals were the indigenous Australians who had lived on the continent for over 65,000 years, long before early Dutch explorers first visited the country in 1770.

We also learnt how British explorer Captain James Cook sailed along the east coast of Australia, later naming it New South Wales (NSW) before claiming this new continent for Great Britain. The British then settled in New South Wales, transporting prisoners to this newly designated penal colony. The first landings were recorded on the 26th January 1788, the date now regarded as Australia Day, which is still celebrated every year across the country.

Following several long discussions with my mum, I finally decided to leave for Australia, going against her wishes. She obviously wanted the best for me and felt that I needed to stay at home and put down some roots, having been away from home since the age of 16. The other concern was that I'd only been seeing this woman for a short period and therefore didn't really know her at all, but as I really liked her, I eventually decided to go. I understood my mum's concerns – any logic should have told me to stay so I could start carving out a new life – but my heart was telling me to go.

I was driven to Gatwick Airport by my mum, dad, and brother, and after a tearful goodbye I headed off towards the departure gates to jump on the Cathay Pacific flight to Hong Kong. My brother later told me that they all went up to the spectators' gallery to watch my flight take off, standing there for what he said felt like ages as they watched my plane disappear – until it was just a little dot in the sky. Apparently, Mum thought it would be ages before they'd see me again.

After a two-day stopover in Hong Kong, discovering the delights of the city, I boarded the plane for my onward journey to Sydney. I was excited but nervous; after all, I hadn't seen my girlfriend for four months and I didn't know what to expect. I'd always had a safety net around me – first my parents and then the army – but now it dawned on me that I was well and truly on my own, with the added dilemma of being 12,000 miles from home.

I arrived in 1988, when Australia was in the midst of celebrating the bicentenary of the country, marking 200 years since the arrival of the first British convict ships in Sydney during 1788. I was met at the airport by my girlfriend, her dad, and her sister. Still feeling nervous, I entered into a conversation with her sister at first, who was asking about my journey. Fortunately, my girlfriend quickly entered the conversation and the atmosphere soon became relaxed. It took us approximately 40 minutes to arrive in the city, and as we drove over the Sydney Harbour Bridge I remember looking out over this huge, vast harbour – with the Opera House to my right – cementing the fact that I was now in Australia and signalling that I was now officially a long way from home. After a few minutes we arrived at the apartment in Lavender Bay, and after grabbing my bags, the two of us got in the lift.

As the front door opened I could see the vista laid out in front of me – the whole harbour in all its glory, with a park adjacent to the front of the building, Luna Park in the foreground, sitting below the Harbour Bridge, and then the Sydney Opera House against the backdrop of a mass of ferries and yachts on the water. Wow, what a view.

The apartment was basic but perfect – it consisted of a single room with a kitchen and shower, large open windows boasting the beautiful vista, and a double bed in one corner.

It wasn't long before we had reconnected and were getting on like a house on fire. The first few weeks I was playing tourist, being taken to all the sightseeing hotspots including Manly and Bondi beaches, the Opera House, and cruising around the harbour on the famous Sydney Ferries. I got into the local nightlife of North Sydney and Chatswood, soon realising that it was very different to back home, with live rock music being played in most bars every night. It was a very male-dominated environment, with everyone drinking either Fosters or Tooheys lager. I quickly learnt that the Australian phrase, "No worries, mate," was so true.

I had sold my car and raided my savings, arriving in Australia well off, but after a couple of months my savings were being depleted so I decided it was time to find a job – particularly as my girlfriend was not at all interested in working, despite having rent to pay. I initially got a job in a bar, but that meant late nights and having to remove drunken men at the end of the evening – not an easy task when the drinking started early afternoon. I only lasted five days there before joining McDonald's in North Sydney, located just five minutes from my apartment. The job involved early mornings with an early finish – allowing me to carry on with my fitness regime – but more importantly, the working environment was relaxed, being that all the staff were backpackers from all over the world, creating a common thread amongst us.

I started work straight away, opting for the early shift, which entailed getting the restaurant ready for the breakfast rush before moving on to preparing the standard menu ready for lunch. North Sydney was a thriving business district; it was located on the northern shore, with great views overlooking the harbour, and was within walking distance of Milsons Point, where I would spend much of my downtime. I managed to stay away from serving points in my job – as I knew I wouldn't enjoy the face-to-face contact – opting instead to stay back of house, ensuring all stock items were constantly replenished to meet the heavy demand.

Everything that McDonald's taught you was by way of short introductory videos, from hygiene standards to how to wear your uniform, even down to the precise detail of making a Big Mac – how long to cook the patties (burgers), toast the buns, how much lettuce, diced onions, burger sauce... etc. etc. This was effective training that worked. The other ethos embedded into our mindset was, "*If you have time to lean, you've got time to clean,*" therefore allowing the owners to get maximum output from their staff at all times. There were no other employment opportunities on offer, but the working hours were perfect, so I decided to stick it out.

Unfortunately, cracks started appearing in my relationship. I was working all day whilst my girlfriend stayed at home, though she still wanted me to go out most nights – something I couldn't sustain as I didn't have the luxury of being able to stay in bed in the mornings. We also started arguing over irrelevant things, and she started to resent the idea that I wanted to go travelling – even though I kept insisting we should go together. The other factor was her sister, who constantly caused problems by stirring up my girlfriend's emotions, ultimately trying to get her to turn against me. The relationship had turned into a regular cycle of arguing followed by heavy drinking followed by sex. This cycle of events eventually became sour, with even her mother getting involved and turning against me. I continued working right up to the end of the tenancy, at which point we moved into her parents' house prior to travelling. The relationship stayed on the same course, so we both decided a break would be the best thing for both of us.

I packed my backpack and said my goodbyes before heading north by coach to Byron Bay. After a two-day stopover I headed straight up to the Gold Coast for a couple of weeks, enjoying the wonderful surfing beaches and bustling bars. I then continued north through Noosa and Fraser Island, and then all the way up to Airlie Beach before turning around and heading back, settling on Great Keppel Island – located 15 kilometres from the Queensland coast, a ferry ride from Rockhampton. This was a beautiful island boasting white sandy beaches and crystal clear waters over the Great Barrier Reef, the perfect mecca for backpackers.

I remained in contact with my girlfriend, but it soon became clear that she wasn't happy, citing that I'd left her in Sydney with no consideration. This went on for a few days until I could no longer relax, so after some strained telephone calls I decided to fly back to Sydney. On my arrival, I went straight to a youth hostel, where we met up. The atmosphere hadn't really changed; if anything it was even worse, as we were now arguing about my travels and how I'd left her back home. The same pattern of behaviour continued.

The atmosphere was still not good, so I decided to take the coach across to Perth in Western Australia, a trip that took me over two weeks to undertake, jumping off and visiting cities and places of interest en route. I headed straight over to my cousin's house, as she'd offered me a place to stay. She showed me all the best places to visit in Perth – including Kings Park and the Swan River – and I even saw some kangaroos in the local parks. It didn't take long, however, for the phone calls to start and the arguing to commence over the same old issues. This time it got so bad that I told her to jump on a plane and travel across to Perth to be with me, which she did.

For the first few days things started to get better, but before long we were back at square one, with us arguing again. I remained in Perth for a month before we both headed back to Sydney, as Christmas was looming. When we got back we decided that I'd go back to the youth hostel whilst my girlfriend went back to her parents'. Meanwhile, her grandfather had arrived for Christmas, and had quickly joined forces with her mum and sister, continuing to turn her against me. I had now exhausted all my funds and had limited money left, just enough to tide me over for the next month or so. This meant that I had to go back to work, though as I didn't relish the thought of going back to McDonald's, I made the tough decision to go back home for Christmas.

I had totally messed up; I had no money left, which resulted in me having to phone my sister, asking her to purchase my flight so I could get home. This was a hard decision to make. After all, the time I'd spent with the Australian woman in the UK had been great, and I savoured the memories we'd made, so I just couldn't work out why it had gone so wrong. I was gutted, as I still had true feelings for her. I said goodbye to her in a bar in Kirribilli whilst *Teardrops* by Womack & Womack played in the background – fitting. I left Sydney on a cold, wet day, and I vividly remember how upset I was as the plane took off, leaving behind both Sydney and my ex-girlfriend.

17

BACK TO LIFE, BACK TO REALITY

I returned home from Australia in late December, just a few days before Pan Am Flight 103 was blown up over the Scottish town of Lockerbie; a large section of the aircraft landed on a residential street, killing all passengers and crew on board. With a death toll of over 270, this bombing is still the deadliest terror attack to occur in the United Kingdom. My lasting memory of this tragedy was witnessing the front end of the fuselage – the cockpit section – lying fully intact on the ground, in full view.

I had returned home to my dad telling me, "Now it's time to sort your shit out." His perception was that I'd been drifting for the last few months, and he wasn't wrong. It was now 1989, so it was definitely time to get sorted. For the first three months I'd remained in contact with the woman from Australia – including a ten-day return trip back to Sydney to meet up again – but it was clear that we'd both moved on. The record of the year was *Back to Life (However Do You Want Me)* featuring Caron Wheeler and the band Soul II Soul – it was no doubt one of the best tunes of the eighties, summing up exactly how I was feeling at the time. I'd left home at 16 to enter my baptism of fire, I'd had a successful military career – before disappointment made me leave the army suddenly – and then I'd decided to travel to Australia, totally unplanned. So yes, it was time to get back to life and face reality!

I was feeling a little lost, having had to adjust to civilian life, which was proving as alien to me as the army had when I first joined back in 1983. I had only known two things in my life so far: the military and fitness. My army days were over, so I decided that my starting point should be the sport centre and swimming pool where I'd spent most of my childhood. Unfortunately, there were no positions available as these jobs were popular and rarely advertised. So, instead, I decided to follow my dad's advice and apply to British Airways. I was successful at interview and started straight away, initially enjoying working for a company that had the vision to be the best and that offered a smart uniform I could wear with pride. The job paid well and had attractive travel benefits, but it wasn't enough; there was no sport attached to my new job description. I remained at British Airways for 10 months before seeing a position advertised at the sport centre. I jumped at the opportunity.

I arrived at the interview with my polished CV and folder full of qualifications. Prior to the interview I'd had to take a swimming test, likening it to the same one I'd undertaken back in Aldershot, as a pass would guarantee an interview. I really wanted this job, so when I walked into the room to be met by the General Manager and the woman from Human Resources, I made sure that I was full of confidence, looking at them directly in their eyes whilst introducing myself. I talked through my time in the army and specifically my role as the squadron PTI, providing examples of the lessons taught followed by talking about overseas tours. It was clear they were looking for candidates with a sporting background, so I concluded by talking about karate. The club had gone on to establish a strong reputation within the town and any link with them came with kudos, hopefully gaining more recognition.

I left the interview feeling satisfied as they both seemed impressed with my performance, and as I walked home –screaming out with excitement – I was the same boy I'd been driving up to Port Stanley, full of confidence and totally ecstatic. The job offer came a few days later in the post, and there was no debate to be had. I had the conversation with my dad – who appeared to be disappointed, as he felt I had better prospects at the airport – but I was adamant. I knew my own mind, so I would just have to prove him wrong, remembering too well his comments when I'd returned from Australia.

After serving my one month's notice, I commenced work at the sport centre. My first priority was to qualify as a lifeguard – which involved passing the Bronze Medallion test so that I could work poolside without supervision – and after a two-week training course I was ready for the test. I was advised that it was a difficult test to pass, but almost impossible if I got an examiner referred to as 'Claire the Clipboard'.

With our training complete, we sat next to the pool awaiting the arrival of the examiner, watching in disbelief as a lady walked in with a clipboard under her arm. We all looked at each other, obviously thinking the same thing: we were all destined to fail. I tried my hardest, but as expected, none of us met her standard. I likened her to the instructors on the Junior Military Qualification Certificate, who never allowed you to pass any test or inspection first time, making you even more determined on your next attempt. I retook the test two weeks later, this time passing and allowing me to work without supervision. I settled into the job quickly, really enjoying the job variety and making new friends in the process. At last, I was starting to put down some permanent roots in my home town.

There was news coming out of Germany that the Berlin Wall had fallen. Following a series of revolutions in Eastern Bloc countries, vast crowds of East Germans started congregating at the wall before deciding to climb onto the structure to meet up with West Germans on the other side, this act being recognised as the start of the fall of the wall. I had last visited East Berlin in the German Democratic Republic (GDR), entering through the only entry point at the time known as Checkpoint Charlie in West Berlin. The fall of the wall led to the German reunification months later, which is cited as the end of the Cold War. This was significant as I had lived through the Cold War for over 18 months, and was left wondering what would happen to the role of the British Army in Germany in the future.

The nineties were now upon us. The eighties had been defining for me, having started the decade at school as a wayward skinhead, then going on to achieve my early ambitions of attaining black belt in Kyokushinkai Karate, and then passing army selection before going on to serve all over the world. I had then travelled to Australia before returning home, eventually finding my dream job. I vividly remember the torch song of the year released in early January from an unassuming 23-year-old Sinead O'Connor, whose performance on *Top of the Pops* made her an overnight star with her classic track, *Nothing Compares 2U*.

The nineties started with Nelson Mandela being released from prison – after serving 27 years – before going on to become President of South Africa, changing the country's political landscape forever. I would get to visit South Africa years later on expedition with the Army Cadet Force and Combined Cadet Forces.

The other significant change was Margaret Thatcher stepping down after an 11-year tenure. She had been at the helm of the country during my teenage years, being involved with both the Iranian embassy siege and the Falklands War.

I went on to have my first ever blind date in February of the new decade. I'd been paired up with an aerobics instructor from a neighbouring town; we were put together by a mutual friend who considered us to be a good match. She was a military child who'd grown up attending private schools around Wiltshire due to her father being posted to that area with the Royal Air Force (RAF). She was at the top of her profession, and she'd decided to relocate to Sussex, to carry on with her studies and to further her career.

I had just finished a workout at the Gatwick Hilton and was waiting for my friend to finish his shift, so that he could drive me to the pub where we'd arranged to meet. As I waited in the bar area of the hotel I got talking to a man; he introduced himself as Phil and said he was going to the same pub I was heading to. I couldn't work out whether he was trying it on or being genuine, but before I knew it, the three of us were en route to meet my blind date. At least I had safety in numbers.

She had the same idea, as when I arrived she was sitting with a large group of her friends and holding a red rose. I soon learnt that it wasn't intended for me; she'd been given it moments earlier. Shit, I thought – I either had competition in the room or it was a clever tactic. We hit it off straight away, with Phil playing matchmaker. In fact, he turned out to be a great catalyst as he kept the drinks flowing all evening whilst acting as mediator with a running commentary. We all ended up back at her house for a spontaneous party, and it turned out to be a really good night. The relationship lasted for just over three years, ending amicably with our careers taking the blame.

I continued to settle in well to the job, taking on additional responsibilities from the outset and being put forward for a supervisor's course straight away. I also took additional coaching qualifications, adding more experience to my portfolio and allowing job variety to continue, which included teaching mixed keep-fit, boxercise classes, and gym instruction. All the staff had a sporting background and were well-disciplined, allowing a work hard, play hard environment to be established. They all shared a collective mindset too – with the discipline that sport gave them underpinning this work ethos. The camaraderie that I'd become well accustomed to in the army had now started to return in spades.

I managed to establish myself at work through an impromptu incident that happened in the staff room. There was a welterweight boxer at work who was regarded as a good fighter, but he was smug and far too sure of himself, thinking he was the real deal. Whilst on a work break, he walked in wearing boxing gloves and threw another pair to me. I wasn't interested, as I was new and didn't want to jeopardise my job, but he started jabbing me in the face and messing around until he struck me really hard. With that I thought 'fuck it' and decided to throw on the gloves.

We stood toe to toe, trading blows, and he was good – he kept catching me with body and head shots until he hit me square on the nose. That was it: I saw red, and the milling installed during basic training automatically took over, as if I was on autopilot. I responded by continually returning body and head shots until he was flat on his back. He eventually got up, shook my hand, and walked away. Needless to say, he didn't ask me for a rematch.

I continued being put forward for training courses, realising that staying in the same place had its benefits – a lesson I'd previously learnt in the army by missing out on courses and promotions. I obtained further sporting qualifications, which allowed me to teach more activities whilst earning extra money in the process. I also undertook the leisure supervisor's course, which proved decisive as when the new team leader's roles were advertised I gained my first promotion, being given responsibility for a small team. This promotion caused some ill feeling but I rode the storm and remained positive, and it wasn't too long before most people had accepted the decision.

I'd learnt from the army that in order to gain any type of respect, you had to give it first, remaining firm – but fair – whilst allowing no one to take advantage. I adopted this approach straight away, and it wasn't long before my team were performing well and working hard. After a few more months I'd progressed into a management role, allowing me to carry on teaching sporting classes and giving me the best of both worlds.

I carried on this role for three years, really enjoying being part of the management team and taking on more responsibility as it presented itself. Following a second restructure across the business, I was asked to become part of a new management team at a community-based leisure centre sited on the other side of town. It was a much smaller operation with a focus on working with the community; the area was known for having a few problem families and latchkey kids.

The centre was located next door to a youth club, which was fine – until it closed its doors, as this gave the latchkey kids the green light to enter our side and create havoc. They were hostile, and any previous relationships had long since broken down. It was explained to me that I had to try to work with these individuals, win their trust, and get them to work with us – ultimately, to respect our staff and the building. It was clear to me that this was going to be a 'hearts and minds' role. Fortunately, I knew how to make this work and what to do to get the kids on our side, having undertaken this type of role in Belize. I appreciated the importance of reaching out to communities, making direct contact in order to gain trust.

I also knew the importance and power that sport had, particularly as sport had managed to retain many of society's core values that had been lost elsewhere, such as discipline and respect. The latchkey kids were streetwise and showed a lot of bravado, although I knew most were only playing at it. I needed a strong connection that would encourage them to come into the centre and engage in a positive manner. I could then start to work on initiatives that would give them a sense of achievement and the self-pride they deserved to have.

The Barcelona 1992 Olympics had been upstaged by the United States basketball team, who quickly became known as the 'Dream Team'. They were recognised as the first team of professional players to participate in an Olympic Games – all playing in the National Basketball Association (NBA) – and it wasn't long before they were cited as the greatest sporting team ever to be brought together. They went on, as predicted, to win gold after beating Croatia in the final with players Michael Jordan, Scottie Pippen, and Charles Barkley going on to gain superstar status. Basketball was immediately projected into the stratosphere, becoming really popular. It was now a credible sport to be associated with, both on the street and on the indoor courts. Great – I now had the large hook I needed to entice these kids.

With my USP (Unique Selling Point) and my ambition – to attract the latchkey kids – identified, I decided to get straight on with the marketing strategy. I wanted to start with a big event with a star player, so in order to make this happen I obtained local sponsorship, allowing it to be widely advertised. I managed to attract an England player to host the event – being that Michael Jordan was out of the question! – and I eventually settled for a full weekend event culminating in a three on three street tournament, with all attendees receiving a basketball courtesy of the sponsors.

I was pleased that over 90 kids attended the weekend event, and even more pleased that I managed to attract the latchkeys I'd been targeting. The positive news for me was that the targeted kids really enjoyed the two days; they were in the winning team but, more importantly, they appreciated the sense of belonging. This eventually led to regular weekly sessions, and I even managed to retain the England player to keep the momentum going.

I was now on a first-name basis with all the boys, and they were coming into the centre on a regular basis – no longer causing problems but actually wanting to be helpful, waiting around for the next basketball session. The weekly sessions went from strength to strength, leading to the formation of junior teams and leagues that are still operating today. By adopting the 'hearts and minds' philosophy I'd witnessed years earlier by reaching out with a popular activity, I allowed lost trust to be regained whilst also giving the kids a purpose. More importantly, the sessions restored respect between the staff and the kids. Yet again, you should never underestimate the power of sport.

During the same period, I met Jayne again (I had taken her out years earlier whilst seeing her out and about in the wine bar). I was seeking an aerobics instructor to take over a weekly class, not realising that the number I'd been given was hers. She couldn't do the class due to other commitments, but now that we'd made contact again, we started seeing each other.

18

POACHER TURNED GAMEKEEPER

Our first child was born in 1995 on St. Andrew's Day, cementing his name, Andrew – after Jayne's dad. Over the next couple of years I would sell my own house and move in full-time with Jayne and Andrew.

Before long, a new promotion came my way following a change in legislation. Compulsory competitive tendering (CCT), which had been introduced by Margaret Thatcher, allowed private companies to bid and win service contracts that were traditionally managed by local councils. Over the past seven years I had gained vast experience and knowledge, covering all aspects of the business and allowing success at the interview. The role included managing the newly appointed management contractor (operator), ensuring their compliance with the service contract. Initially, I'd been gutted with this change, as we were likened to a close family who were all about to be split up. I decided from the outset, however, that instead of treating this change as a failure, I would turn it into an opportunity. One door had now closed – the job that I loved gone – but that had now allowed a new door to open.

I knew I was going to be in for a busy six months, I decided to call up my army friend (whom I'd met on Exercise Lionheart) and suggested we should go on holiday before the main work started. It had been ten years since I'd served in Belize, so we both decided on a return trip to Cancun. We had a great two weeks there, spending plenty of time in bars, and on the beach doing water sports. By now Cancun had transformed into a global destination, and was barely recognisable from when we'd been there before.

143

As expected, the first month proved difficult, mobilising the new contract. My new boss was ambitious, demanding high standards at all times and running her department like a military operation. An international sportswoman representing Great Britain in her respected sport, she combined her disciplined sporting approach into her work ethic.

Having allowed a period of time for the new operator to settle in, we undertook the first inspection of the centres. My boss, however, was not happy, stating that the service was below standard and that I was to convey this message to the manager. I'd sort of expected this, considering that the first question at my interview had been: *"How are you going to turn from Poacher into Gamekeeper?"*

This proved to be a difficult conversation – as he'd been a good mentor, helping to establish my career – but it simply had to be done. Fortunately, he respected my approach. The manager soon moved on, which is often the case with any management takeover, and this certainly made my approach easier: now I could be totally objective.

The department had responsibility for all sport across the town – including sport centres, outdoor sports pitches, golf courses, and theatres – and the council were in the process of constructing a new football stadium courtesy of a land deal completed two years earlier. With the opening planned for the 31st August, I was brought into the team to assist with making the final arrangements. The event was planned to be a celebration of sport for the town; it would be a large civic party with the guest of honour being the Minister of Sport.

On the day of the event I remember being woken up during the early hours by my brother, who was phoning me to tell me to turn on the television. When I did, I saw the breaking news confirming that Diana, Princess of Wales had died in a car crash in Paris whilst fleeing the paparazzi. I found this utterly devastating and unbelievable, especially as I'd only been watching her on the news the previous day.

We met early to start the proceedings, as news from the top was that the event was still planned to go ahead. This was new territory; communication was sparse, and what was being conveyed appeared to be rapidly changing. Football teams were ready to play, the caterers and the Red Devils parachute display team booked (although we were unsure if the Minister of Sport was arriving), and so we carried on making the final preparations. It was clear as the morning went on that the political landscape was changing quickly, and finally the decision was made to cancel. We closed the stadium, contacted the relevant organisations, and put out communications before going home, where I found myself glued to the television, watching the events of the day unfold.

The sudden death of Princess Diana led to many tributes and public offerings of cards, messages, candles, and flowers being left outside both Buckingham Palace and Kensington Palace. I even visited Buckingham Palace the following week with Jayne to pay our respects. As we stood outside the palace we could start to see a media frenzy occur between CNN and ITV News, just as a bright light suddenly appeared up at one of the windows, signalling that the Queen was about to address the waiting nation during a live broadcast. Soon after the broadcast, we watched as Prince Charles and Princes William and Harry left the palace in a motorcade. Less than a week after her death, the nation stood silent as the funeral took place in London in front of a global television audience. The stadium opened less than two months later, with a great civic event and the Red Devils delivering the match ball – just as planned.

I had now settled into my job, with a variety of work now coming in spades. I started working on key projects, beginning with the development of a skate park – with the intention of moving skateboarders away from the town centre. Following recent redevelopment work, architects had created superb riding lines, jumps, and exciting features – making it a perfect mecca for any skateboarding enthusiast – and I quickly learnt the process, consultation, design, tendering, and then appointment. I excelled in this area of work, eventually going on to bigger projects.

Luke was born during August, a summer baby, making our family complete. We were both convinced we were going to have a girl so it came as a nice surprise – though the name we'd chosen, Beth, had to be quickly replaced. It took two weeks to come up with a new name that we both liked, eventually settling on Luke.

The 90s were coming to an end, and we were fast approaching the new Millennium. I can vividly remember talking about the Year 2000 whilst at school when it seemed light years away, and now it was actually only weeks away – something that left me thinking, 'where had the time gone?!' We were tasked with ensuring all buildings and services did not fall victim to the Millennium bug, also referred to as the Y2K bug, which was poised to cause havoc all over the world on New Year's Eve, 1999. The problem was in the coding of computer systems poised to attack all computer networks, including aircraft – where some reports suggested they could even fall out of the sky.

We spent New Year's Eve at home, watching the Y2K bug work its way across the world with little or no impact, as had been feared by so many. We then stayed up to watch the fireworks over London, before going to bed in preparation for our impending visit to the Millennium Dome.

The new century brought new opportunities for the town, and I positioned myself to become a key player in these developments. The sport centres had been built around the time of the new town and were no longer viable, costing hundreds of thousands of pounds to operate. The town had a proud history of sport, and had therefore positioned itself as a sporting town. Due to an expansion in the private fitness sector, however – and then regional facilities starting to spring up – the town had lost market edge, so now it was time to respond!

A sports strategy commenced to identify the needs of the town, which included extensive consultations to inform the design brief. It was clear from the outset that the council wanted to put the town back on the map, and in order to achieve this, the new facilities would need to fulfil the sporting needs at local, regional, and national levels. Fortunately, we had the vision to make this happen.

The England rugby team were just about to put sport back at the top of the agenda again, which was great timing and which added weight to our business case. Like Alf Ramsey before him, Sir Clive Woodward masterminded another sporting first by winning the Rugby World Cup. England had arrived in Australia as favourites to win, having been ranked number one in the world, and when they met Australia – the former world champions – in their back yard for the final, they won 20-17, courtesy of the famous drop goal by Jonny Wilkinson in the final seconds of the match.

Sir Clive Woodward stated that training with the Royal Marines was key to his side winning the 2003 Rugby World Cup; the Marine culture embedded into the squad during 1999 had taken hold within the England camp, in readiness for 2003. The mindset taught by the Marines was based on attitude and how this impacts the whole team, citing that one wrong player would zap the energy from everyone else. Following the disappointment of the 1999 World Cup, Woodward implemented the lessons learnt from the Marines to good effect.

The scheme would have to stack up financially in terms of both construction and running costs, as well as creating a strong brand within the marketplace. As we had experience of doing land deals, relocating the centre to a new location seemed the obvious choice to generate funds, making the scheme viable. We decided, therefore, to present a really ambitious business case, which caused concern within certain quarters – with some people stating the project was too far-reaching and likely not achievable.

They say timing is everything, and this was the case when two key factors came into play, giving the project a much-needed boost: the local education authority was in the process of building a school identified as a 'specialist sports college', and London was being put forward as host city for the 2012 Olympics.

Consultation was undertaken over 18 months, informing the design brief and allowing for a tangible project to be developed. A deal was then completed, realising the land value of the existing sport centre and allowing the new facility to be constructed on the same site as the specialist sports school. The success lay with the design team, who had the foresight and vision to make this project happen – and who were willing to take the necessary (calculated) risks. Still believing the Olympics to be a real prospect, we really went for it, building a centre that would have national significance. Construction commenced, and the new facility was finished in just under two years.

We broke the mould, constructing an Olympic-standard facility at zero cost; the land deal covered all construction costs, and the new centre – which would open in late November – would even go on to save hundreds of thousands of pounds.

I went up to London to watch the International Olympic Committee (IOC) award the 2012 Olympics to the host city on the big screen at Trafalgar Square; the vote was undertaken in Singapore and beamed live all across the world. After watching countries being discounted one by one, London was eventually successful, winning the right to host the 2012 Olympic Games and beating long-term favourites Paris in the process. It was reported that it was extremely close, with only four votes in it.

When the announcement was made, the whole of Trafalgar Square went wild, while – simultaneously – the Red Arrows flew over the square, trailing their trademark red, white, and blue smoke. As I watched the smoke trails above, all I could do was cry tears of joy; all the hard work had certainly been worth it, especially knowing that we'd proved the doubters wrong and were now relishing the reality that the Olympics were coming to London.

The celebrations were short-lived, however, as London went from total euphoria to complete devastation in less than 24 hours. Four suicide bombers carrying rucksacks full of explosives attacked the city, killing 52 people and injuring hundreds more. The attacks known as 7/7 took place on three underground trains around Edgware Road, Aldgate, and Russell Square, as well as on a double-decker bus in Tavistock Square.

Mum & Dad - Wedding Day - 1961

Standing tall with my sister on her wedding day - 1987

Our favourite skiing destination - Pas de la Casa

Looking out - Mont Blanc Massif

Summit photo – Mont Blanc

Tower of London with Luke

Enjoying the vista - Everest Base Camp

Departing Lukla airport with Andrew

Pen Y Fan with Jayne

Favourite spot – Tenerife

Mont Teide Massif with my brother Steve

Me and Jayne

Topping Out Lake District – Wast Water in shot

Empty ski resort - Covid strikes. Austria

19

SUMMIT FEVER

The new sport centre was performing beyond all expectations, having quickly established itself as a community facility with national significance. Due to the impeccable timing, the town had made strong links with the London Organising Committee of the Olympic and Paralympic Games (LOCOG), which was charged with the planning and development of the 2012 Games.

Sebastian Coe – Chair of London 2012 – agreed to be guest of honour at the official opening, with the icing on the cake being when the centre was selected as a pre-training camp for international athletes to utilise during the build-up to the games. The 2012 design team also visited the facility to share future ideas for the Olympic Park. With managing the portfolio of facilities, work continued to remain busy as we strove to attain higher standards all the time, and I'd also gained a further promotion following an internal restructure, helped by the delivery of the successful leisure project. The work, however, wasn't done yet; we still had many tough challenges ahead.

Negotiations followed, resulting in us achieving a break-even position where we agreed to manage the new facilities for a three-year period. This switch was a real game changer, having gone from a service costing hundreds of thousands of pounds to now achieving a cost neutral position on the management fee (payment to operator).

Personally, I was in a good place; I realised that I'd definitely made the right career choice years earlier when I'd followed my dad's strong words of advice: "sort your shit out". I had certainly done that, and I'd done it by proving him wrong; by not staying at British Airways like he'd wanted me to. I had taken all the skills I'd learnt from karate and the army, and had continued to adopt the same mindset in the pursuit of my career. The leisure project was deemed a great success, mostly due to the team all sharing the same ambition and determination to make it happen. There was quite a bit of risk, failures to overcome, good timing, and some luck involved, but most of all, a collective resolve to keep going despite all the many setbacks.

I was formally recognised for my efforts and, as a result, was awarded funding towards a personal development programme. I wasn't at all interested in any of the conventional courses on offer, however, so I decided to opt for a week's winter mountaineering course in North Wales, stating that this training would be far more beneficial – I'd just hoped the Human Resources Manager would buy it, and fortunately, he did!

My 40th birthday was fast approaching, and I'd decided to celebrate by doing something special. I wanted to set myself a challenge that would push me to my limits, being that it had been quite some time since I'd done anything with any real risk attached. As I'd always enjoyed the mountains, I decided to set myself the goal of reaching the summit of Mont Blanc – Western Europe's highest mountain, standing at over 4,800 metres high.

This was going to be a difficult technical climb as it was high on the snow line and it required walking in crampons, as well as having to competently utilise an ice axe whilst being tied to another climber by rope – all whilst potentially battling altitude mountain sickness. With this in mind, I decided that Snowdon would be the perfect training ground, as – during February in particular – it is widely recognised for its harsh environment.

So, as planned, I arrived in Snowdonia early February. It was cold, there was snow on the ground, and it was also really windy. As I stepped off the train and looked around me, the thought of a regular training course sounded like a much better option, but those thoughts soon disappeared as my taxi pulled up. This was going to be a tough five days in testing conditions, particularly with the snow on the ground making even basic skills difficult, but I was ready for the challenge. The joining instructions identified the key objectives as 'learning how to remain safe and comfortable in changeable conditions whilst getting to grips with specialist skills and equipment'. A good standard of fitness was deemed a prerequisite as we were told to expect long, hard days covering both long distances and heights.

As expected, the week proved difficult as I mastered new skills such as avalanche awareness, weather recognition, self-arrest, and navigation – all the challenges that would be waiting for me on Mont Blanc. Our mountain guide was a first-rate climber whose own skills were soon to be fully tested. Throughout the week I'd learnt how to walk in crampons, as well as learning basic rope work and ice axe techniques including the self-arrest, where you had to fall down a steep descent on the mountainside on your back, place the ice axe across your body, then turn over quickly onto your front whilst sticking the axe into the snow, eventually bringing you to a stop. This practice was exhausting, but as it was a technique that saved many lives, we kept going over it again and again until we'd mastered it.

During day three we were climbing up a steep ascent, working our way up towards the summit of Tryfan – standing at 918 metres – and walking in deep snow tied in by rope when, suddenly, the stunning scenery around us disappeared in seconds, being replaced by thick cloud. Visibility was reduced down to nothing; you could barely see the person in front of you. Standing on a steep incline with snow on the ground and zero visibility – our surroundings now totally featureless – was a scary place to be.

The first thing the guide did was to bring us together; he reduced the lengths of our ropes, ensuring we stuck close to each other, then he told us to take control of our ice axes, reminding everyone of the self-arrest drill we'd been taught earlier before informing us that we were going to continue up towards the summit. He pulled out his map and compass, worked out where we were before setting a bearing, and with that we headed upwards into the dark abyss. I was sort of hoping we were going to abort and head back down, but he was adamant we would make it to the summit, so it was a case of head down and dig deep, my right hand firmly gripping my ice axe. We were then introduced to a recognised mountaineering term, 'total whiteout', which proved terrifying as we climbed higher and higher on the precarious steep slope.

When we were approximately 100 metres from the summit, the cloud suddenly disappeared and we were once again treated to the fantastic vista laid out in front of us. It really was amazing watching the guide using his navigational skills whilst ensuring we all remained safe, and the skills I learnt during those five days would prove vital when I stepped out onto the mountains around Chamonix.

My next trip was a week in Munich with a group of friends to celebrate my upcoming birthday; it coincided with the 2006 World Cup, and we made good use of the Fan Zones dotted throughout the city. The Fan Zones were great – they featured huge television screens, plenty of bars, and a real party atmosphere with people from all over the world. This was my first time back in Germany since 1986, when the Berlin Wall had still been standing and the Cold War was being played out between East and West, and I couldn't believe how much the world had changed over the previous 10 years. It was a brilliant week and a great way to remember my 40th year, but I wasn't done yet: Mont Blanc was looming fast.

I arrived in Chamonix a couple of days before the climb as I wanted to get some much-needed rest beforehand; I had read about how altitude sickness posed a real threat, so I knew that a relaxed and strong mindset was required. It had been widely reported that people trying to reach the summit had just a 50%

success rate, with the reasons for failure cited as a lack of fitness, altitude sickness, and inclement weather. My other reason for arriving early was that the town of Chamonix sits at over 1,000 metres above sea level, allowing my body time to start acclimatising to the altitude.

So, after spending two days acclimatising in Switzerland by sleeping at over 3,000 metres above sea level, and after practising the same mountain skills I'd learnt back in Wales, we headed to Chamonix for the summit attempt. The weather in Switzerland had not been good – with storms affecting our training programme – but the good news was that the forecast for summit day was clear with bright sunshine, making perfect conditions for the ascent. After a hearty breakfast we caught the train up to the start of the climb before setting off on the two-hour walk up to the first rest stop for the night, the Tête Rousse Hut. Once there, it was heads down and rest – the next two days were going to be long and hard.

After a restless sleep in Tête Rousse, we got up at around 3 a.m. to commence the climb up Mont Blanc; we got dressed and grabbed our equipment before assembling at the back of the hut to receive our safety briefing. It was freezing, and I remember looking up towards the Goûter Hut, watching a line of head torches scaling the vertical rock face high above us. In order to reach the starting point of the climb, we first had the challenge of crossing the Grand Couloir, a large precarious gully with a reputation for being a notorious accident black spot. In fact, this area is sometimes referred to as the 'gully of death' due to the many fatal accidents recorded there, with some commentators actually comparing it to a game of Russian roulette. We were told to make the traverse as quickly as possible, as stonefall is often channelled down the couloir, making it even more dangerous. Needless to say, the traverse was made in super quick time.

We were in a group of 12 climbers, all new to this type of exposure, which actually gave me some comfort knowing that we were all about the same level and that we were all in this together. There were two climbers attached to each guide by a safety rope, with the guide taking the central position, allowing me to be lead person. It was still pitch-black when we left, with our head torches as the only light source. It was time to go.

The route up to the Goûter Hut was the most technical part of the climb, requiring us to scramble up the rock face on all fours while using our arms to pull ourselves onwards and upwards. After two hours of hard scrambling we reached the hut – where we were instructed to leave certain items of equipment behind to reduce the weight in our backpacks – before having some food and drink and then quickly heading off again. It was clear that time was of the essence. Our arrival at the hut coincided with sunrise, allowing the snow to sparkle as the brilliant bright white wonderland opened up before us. Then we had one final equipment check before the guide communicated to us, "The real work is just about to start. Remember, small steps at a steady pace; this is the only race in the world where the tortoise beats the hare!"

With that we headed off again, with me leading followed by the guide, then the second climber behind us, all tied to one another. The views were amazing – with the Chamonix Valley to the left and the Dôme du Goûter straight ahead – but before we could start climbing, a steep descent lay before us. The snow was soft on the foot as I started to set the pace, remembering the advice we'd been given a few minutes earlier. After descending, we finally got into the actual climb, signalling that it was going to be all uphill from here on in. The final test was now on, and I definitely felt I had enough in the tank to reach the summit.

During the acclimatisation phase we were told to control any anxiety, keep our heads down, take one step at a time, and – most importantly – break the climb up into small chunks; we were told to forget about the summit and focus on the next section only. For me it was the two peaks of the Dôme du Goûter, which stood at over 4,300 metres, and it wasn't long before I was standing on top of the Dome looking up towards the summit of Mont Blanc. We stopped there for a quick break, having some water before carrying on. By this time one of the party was suffering from a bad headache and consequently had to drop back to rest before being able to push on again.

At this point I started feeling a bit weary myself, and although I started to question my ability, I soon realised that this was now down to my strength of mind, as physically I was smashing it. I continued, but all of a sudden I started to feel nauseous, thinking, *shit, I've got altitude sickness* (apparently this is a common emotion when climbing at altitude; your mind starts playing tricks on you, resulting in you thinking the worst). I had no other option than to push on past the Vallot Hut situated to my left, marking just over 400 metres to the summit.

Heads down, we pushed higher and higher until we reached the final ridge line and hit the summit. We'd done it! As I stood at the summit, over 4,800 metres above sea level, I felt utterly euphoric – it was just such a great achievement in my 40th year. We all sat down on the top, looking down at the 360-degree view of the Alps with the Chamonix Valley below as we drank some much-needed water. I also remember eating a packet of wine gums whilst watching the other climbers arriving. We stayed there for 15 minutes and not a minute longer – otherwise, altitude sickness would start to attack.

Our guide checked us over before telling us that we were only half done; the summit was 50% of the climb and we now had to get back to the start – safely. It was important to stay switched on, as the majority of accidents occur on the way down. I took the advice, looking downhill before stepping out. After two hours we arrived back at the Goûter Hut where we had an hour's rest stop, giving me enough time to have a well-deserved can of Coke and a Mars Bar. It reminded me of how important Mars Bars were for that instant energy boost, having always relied on them whilst on exercise with the army.

A two-hour scramble down the rock face towards Tête Rousse left us with one final challenge before we were home and safe: the Grand Couloir. This time we were doing the traverse in daylight, the risk greater than before as the warm sun had been melting the snow all day, creating regular rockfalls. On the way down, the traverse was almost undertaken as a sprint. The whole thing was a fantastic experience that will remain with me forever.

Fitness was definitely a prerequisite to reach the summit, but mental strength was just as important; without a positive mindset, there was simply no way of reaching the top. Even before the climb, the word 'failure' was well documented within the joining instructions, which had told me about the 50% success rate. I didn't want to be in the half that didn't reach the summit! My deep-rooted training from karate and junior leaders were certainly defining factors in my reaching the top of Europe, though I also mustn't forget that the weather was on my side too.

I was so chuffed with my incredible achievement that I decided to take my family back to Chamonix to show them the mountain close-up, not realising at the time that this trip would influence and go on to shape my older child's future career. We visited Chamonix in early February – the town having been transformed into a winter wonderland – and as it is widely recognised as one of the most popular ski resorts, it felt right to take the family skiing. I had learnt to ski whilst serving in Germany on Exercise Snow Queen – which is undertaken every year in Bavaria – and I'd gained intermediate qualifications. None of my family had ever put on a pair of ski boots, however, so it was time for them to give it a go!

We travelled to Les Houches, which is located at the far end of Chamonix, and found great nursery slopes sitting within the shadows of Mont Blanc. Then, after hiring the equipment, we caught the cable car up to the piste, a vast picture postcard scene. I felt confident I could teach my family the basics, so I gave them a five-minute lesson, quickly explaining the 'snowplough', how to slow down, and how to stop. And with that I was gone – leaving Jayne, Andrew, and Luke behind to figure out how to get down the 200-metre slope laid out in front of them… big mistake!

This was far too much for them, far too soon – my enthusiasm had taken over, and I soon realised this wasn't such a good idea after all. So, I pulled up, caught the button lift back up, checked all was OK, and then went to the shop to book them some lessons. Fortunately, an instructor was on hand to teach them the basics, giving them the confidence they needed to continue over the next few days – with my older son even progressing to snowboarding. That week was a defining moment for Andrew, as from that very first day on the snow, he went on to shape a career working all around the world as a professional snowboarding instructor.

Over the next three years, work continued at pace with new projects coming on board all the time, bringing job variety in spades. The new sport centre was continuing to perform well; by the third year it was hosting both national and international sporting events as well as attracting well over a million visitors per year, recording more visits than London Zoo. It was deemed a great success and is often cited as a benchmark for future schemes. We even entered into a new 10-year contract term, seeking an operator to take the service forward towards the Olympics and beyond.

We had already reached break-even, but – now that we had three years of trading behind us – we wanted to do better, and because of its significance within the marketplace we could now aggressively market the facilities to obtain a better-quality position. Quality was the prerequisite of the tender process, followed closely by cost, ensuring that any operator would have to push the envelope even further than before.

Following a competitive process involving complex negotiations, a new quality operator was appointed, breaking the mould yet again; this operator was employed to take the service forward whilst paying a significant amount of money for the privilege, meaning that leisure facilities which had previously cost money to operate had now been transformed into healthy cash cows.

Now that the new operator had been employed, we were able to focus on the upcoming Olympic Games; after all, we had all the facilities and the right location to make a real difference. At the same time, for some reason I started to miss military life, so I started investigating ways I could get back into the green uniform once again.

20

GIVING BACK

I wanted to return to uniform; after all, I had maintained interest in all things military following the operations in Iraq and Afghanistan in the same way I had the Falklands War. I'd continued to remain busy at work, however, so I therefore didn't have the time or the capacity to join the Army Reserve, opting instead for the Army Cadet Force (ACF). I had enjoyed the Marine Cadets and gained great satisfaction from impacting the young people on the basketball project, so with this in mind I decided it would be my way back into the military environment.

It was social reformer Octavia Hill who formed London's first independent Cadet Battalion – the Southwark Cadet Company – way back in 1889. She believed that the military training would point struggling youths in the right direction, citing: *"There is no organisation which I have found that influences the boys so powerfully for good as that of our cadets... and if such ideas can be brought before the young lad before he gets in with a gang of loafers it may make all the difference to his life."* The title 'Cadet Force' was introduced during 1908, with all administration undertaken by the Territorial Army. By 1914, there had been substantial expansion.

During the Second World War, both the Army Cadets and the Sea Cadets saw further expansion, whilst also laying the foundations for the creation of the Air Training Corps. At the end of the war the Army Cadet Association (ACFA) was formed, with the Combined Cadet Force (CCF) being set up in 1948. With the war now over and national service coming to an end, citizen training was extended to include the piloting of the Duke of Edinburgh's Award (DofE).

I arrived at Quebec Barracks for the adult instructor selection process, knowing that these tests would include fitness testing, command tasks, interviews, and a short presentation to the other candidates. In my presentation I spoke about my job and the link to the upcoming Olympic Games, as well as the positive impact sport could have on their communities by citing how I'd won over the latchkey kids. We were informed that the training would take place over four weekends, culminating – if we were successful, of course – with a seven-day residential camp with the Cadet Training Team. We were going to be taught the cadet military syllabus in preparation for being able to instruct across a range of topics including military knowledge, drill and turnout, fieldcraft, skill at arms, and navigation – skills I'd learnt years earlier. I received notification a week later, confirming that I had been successful and informing me to be ready to report to Crowborough Camp.

I turned up on a Friday night with nine other candidates to commence the training, and we were all introduced to the Officer Commanding, who briefed us on the training programme – stating that we would initially be on probation. Passing the course would then permit passage onto the Army Cadet Instructors Course (ACIC), where success would guarantee the rank of Sergeant Instructor (SI). It was made clear that the ACF was sponsored generously by the Army and therefore subscribed to the Army's values and standards, something that was still very much embedded in my mindset.

The first weekend comprised an introduction to the cadet syllabus by means of team building, drill, physical training, weapon handling, and a navigation exercise over Ashdown Forest. The training was full on – it was like being a recruit again. The next two weekends were just as busy, with us having to learn the Army Proficiency Certificate (APC) – the training syllabus cadets followed – and then leadership training followed by teaching practices in readiness to start instructing lessons. They were the same teaching practices taught on my Junior Military Qualification Certificate (JMQC); as they had hardly changed, I managed to navigate easily and successfully through these lessons.

The early February assessment weekend comprised a two-day fieldcraft introduction at Pippingford Park on tactical exercise. This was a basic introduction to fieldcraft, taking part in camp routine, patrolling, and ambush drills, including two nights under a basha (a shelter) in temperatures well below zero. I got through the training unscathed and gained an overall pass, permitting my passage onto the ACIC. At the same time, I received my first posting to a cadet unit in Sussex.

I started parading twice a week, familiarising myself with the workings of the unit whilst getting to know the instructors and cadets. I commenced with the Basic Training Syllabus, which was initially aimed at brand new cadets and which covered topics such as cadet in the community, drill and turnout, basic fieldcraft, and first aid.

Then – twelve months after the first selection event – I attended the ACIC, arriving at Crowborough Camp for a full week of testing. Instructors from the regular army welcomed us before warning us it was going to be a tough week, starting off with an inspection at 06.30 the next morning – shit! This felt just like the JMQC I had undertaken back in Colerne.

We all failed the inspection – it *was* the JMQC! – and this was followed by physical training and then two hours on the drill square, learning to move as a squad again. We spent the afternoon and evening doing skill at arms and map reading before spending what felt like hours preparing for the next morning's inspection. The week continued with yet more inspections, many hours on the drill square, skill at arms, and instructing basic lessons. We then deployed on an overnight fieldcraft exercise, learning advanced ambush drills and section attacks, ending up with an escape and evasion task. The final day was taken up with testing – a drill lesson, map and compass, and weapon familiarisation. I was given the 'Right turn at the halt' to teach – the same movement I'd had to teach on my JMQC – again, smashing it. This was followed by my last two exams, gaining a pass and allowing my promotion to SI.

I returned to my unit teaching straight away, and it soon became apparent that many cadets were wayward, with some coming from broken homes; having been a wayward child myself, I could really empathise with these young people. The organisation provided the most vulnerable with some security and a belonging, the discipline making a real difference to their lives. Some of the best performing cadets had even been expelled from school, which was hard to believe given their positive attitude whilst attending the unit.

The cadet journey took approximately five years to complete, starting with the Basic Training Syllabus and progressing through 1 to 4 star proficiency levels before succeeding to Master Cadet. Throughout these proficiency levels, cadets are taught a range of military subjects before progressing onto cadres – where cadets are taught how to teach new entrants – before they become eligible for the senior cadres, where they increase their knowledge base to teach basic lessons with a greater focus on leadership. By the time a young person has completed the cadet journey to Master Cadet, they will have covered the military syllabus that army recruits are taught through their basic training, providing them with a clear advantage if they choose to embark on a military career.

The 150th Anniversary of the Cadet Forces was celebrated in 2010, with 150 separate events taking place across the country. The main event took place on the 6th July with a garden party in the grounds of Buckingham Palace, with the Prince of Wales in attendance. I attended the event with my dad, son, sister, and nephew, and we all had a fantastic day out walking around the magnificent grounds, eating cucumber sandwiches, and witnessing first-hand the splendour of this famed palace.

The ACF encourages adventure training alongside the military syllabus, endorsing the Duke of Edinburgh Award Scheme (DofE). I decided, therefore, to extend my skill set in order to gain additional qualifications, especially being that I'd enjoyed the outdoors ever since stepping out with the Fort George Volunteers at age sixteen. So, I undertook the DofE Leadership course, which allowed me to start teaching basic skills and to take cadets on expeditions whilst they worked towards their Bronze and Silver awards. I really enjoyed this element of training; it was a break from the military syllabus whilst also being able to learn new skills.

I enrolled on and passed the Summer Mountain Foundation Course (SMF) held in the Lake District. This was then followed by a tough week in Scotland on the Winter Mountain Foundation (WMF) during February, walking high above the snow line, building snow holes, learning avalanche awareness, and revisiting the self-arrest technique I'd learnt back in Wales. These were long days covering extended distances in harsh winter conditions.

I brought these new skills back to the unit and started introducing the DofE syllabus, adding more credence to a young person's curriculum vitae. Around this time I was also made aware that the ACF were advertising for instructors to participate in a three-week expedition to South Africa. As it would cover the whole country, I knew competition would be fierce. To gain further experience, therefore, I enrolled onto an Alpine Mountaineering course based in Switzerland, hopefully adding more weight to my application.

I attended the weekend selection event, which was held at Halton Training Camp located in Lancaster, on the edge of the Lake District – I had spent a week at this camp back in Junior Leaders, so it felt good to be back there, although I remembered getting stuck upside down in a canoe on a nearby river whilst undertaking capsize drills. Fortunately, there were no water-based activities this weekend. I worked hard over the two days before being offered a position alongside 12 other instructors and 49 cadets.

I set off for South Africa when the London 2012 Games were on, and I was sad that I wasn't going to be in the country for the full duration of the Olympics, especially as I'd been so involved since London winning the right to host the games back in Trafalgar Square. We all met for deployment in Surrey on 'Super Saturday', recognised as the greatest day of the London Games – it was the day in which Great Britain won twelve gold medals, culminating with Jessica Ennis winning gold in the women's heptathlon, Greg Rutherford in the men's long jump, and Mo Farrah in the men's 10,000 metres, all in front of the packed London Stadium. What a night! It was certainly a memorable day, allowing the expedition party to leave the country on a massive high.

When we landed in Johannesburg it was absolutely freezing, especially as we'd just left the warm sunshine of England behind us before arriving in the middle of winter in South Africa – the country was experiencing freak weather, with snow showers throughout Johannesburg, something not witnessed in many years. We then travelled to Ithala National Park to commence the acclimatisation phase, allowing our bodies to start adapting to both the altitude and the environment. This was followed by a two-day walking safari with armed rangers, seeking out the amazing wildlife within the National Park.

We were instructed by rangers that, when approached by any animal, we should stand still and await further instruction. We had only been walking for a couple of hours when we suddenly heard rustling sounds coming from the dense undergrowth, and then – out of nowhere – a black rhino charged out from the bush straight towards us. The ranger shouted, *"Run!"* whilst making lots of noise and aiming his rifle at the animal. We split up, deciding to run off in all directions, and the rhino veered away and ran off into the distance, this apparently being normal for black rhinos. We were later told by the ranger that they can be easily persuaded to abort a charge. I was more concerned that we were told to stand still, only then to be told to run for our lives!

This incident was then followed by what was the most memorable part of the expedition: travelling to Kwazulu-Natal to witness the battlefield of Isandlwana before trekking to Rorke's Drift along the Fugitives' Trail. The last battlefield tour I'd undertaken was on Mt Longdon in the Falkland Islands – a battle that had taken place in 1982 – but now I was standing on a battlefield where events had taken place in January 1879, under the reign of Queen Victoria.

The Battle of Isandlwana was one of the first engagements of the Anglo-Zulu Wars, where approximately 20,000 Zulu warriors – armed only with spears – attacked a contingent of approximately 1,800 British troops. The British were armed with rifles and two 7-pounder mountain guns, but despite this vast advantage, the Zulus overwhelmed the Column, killing over 1,300 troops. This battle still remains the single greatest defeat of the British Army at the hands of a Native Army.

The Battle of Rorke's Drift followed the next day, with the successful British defence of a mission station under the command of John Chard of the Royal Engineers. During this battle, a large section of Zulus broke away from their main force during the final hours of the Battle of Isandlwana to attack Rorke's Drift, located six miles from Isandlwana.

150 British and colonial troops defended the station against repeated attacks from 3,000 to 4,000 Zulu warriors. The British repelled attack after attack, eventually defending the station. For the bravery shown defending the mission station, 11 Victoria Crosses were awarded.

We then left for the two-day training trek, including an overnight stay in Aasvoelkrans Cave. Routes involved the ascent and descent of steep ground, which made for rugged walking, with familiarisation skills taking place on steep terrain and thick tussock grass. This proved vital as it got us walking carrying weight, allowing our bodies to start acclimatising to the higher altitude – and bringing back the important lessons I'd learnt on Mont Blanc. We were now ready for the next phase: walking and wild camping throughout the Drakensberg Mountain range.

The five-day trek included the ascent of the Langalibalele Pass, which we knew was going to be hard as we were carrying five litres of water and food for five days, our pack weight exceeding 25kg. We spent the first day climbing up the long pass before descending into Lesotho to make camp for the night. As we erected tents in the strong winds, local herd boys dressed only in blankets kept wandering over with their wild dogs to watch us.

We got up early the next morning to start the high level traverse of Giant's Castle, ending in a camp on its flank above the Loteni Cutback. The ascent of Giant's Castle followed, summiting early afternoon, when we stood on the summit at 3,316 metres. We'd made it – the whole group managed to reach the top. We camped just below the summit before descending Giant's Pass, and the final two days were spent traversing the long Contour path, finishing at Mountain Shadows for a well-earned rest. The five days proved testing for the cadets, giving them the invaluable experience of living and trekking in remote areas on demanding mountain terrain.

Everyone was then rewarded with two days' Rest and Recuperation (R&R) at the Bushwillow Tented Camp, enjoying the use of spa pools whilst interacting with the local monkeys. We also visited a crocodile farm before finishing up being entertained by a traditional South African braai (barbeque) and Beggar's Opera put on by the cadets, allowing them the opportunity to ridicule the leadership team.

The Community phase was the most rewarding element for all members of the expedition, which was when we undertook five days of work at the Insonge Community Primary School, located two miles from where we were staying – at some converted stables at the Entabeni Outdoor Centre. This was a Zulu school for children from the local area, and they all greeted us with huge smiles every morning after the forty-minute walk in. My group worked on the construction and fitting of blackboards into classrooms before fitting new toilets in the newly constructed block. The toilets were basic – just a hole in the ground – and as previous groups had installed the drainage, it was down to us to make the final connections. The cadets had never witnessed such basic living conditions, with most being deeply moved by what they'd experienced over those five days. The Zulu children were well behaved despite having nothing – not even shoes on their feet – and they were happy, with stress nowhere to be seen!

Within two years I was back on national expedition, this time in Kenya to undertake a school construction project, as well as climbing, white water rafting, and attempting the ascent of Mount Kenya. This time I would be staring failure in the face again whilst climbing high on Mount Kenya.

The first 17 miles were covered walking up an unmarked track until we reached Elephant Clearings, a well-known location for spotting wild elephants. Halfway into the trek, however, it started to rain, turning the track into a muddy quagmire and making it a hard slog on foot for the remainder of the day. We finally arrived, quickly pitching our tents to escape the rain. It was during this period that I started to lose my appetite and feel nauseous. I took on water then went to sleep, hoping to shake off whatever I had picked up. I remembered eating what I felt was raw meat whilst back at the first camp; I had bitten into a piece of meat that felt soft and cold, although – at the time – I'd dismissed it.

I woke up still feeling rough, but I pushed on with the main party, just managing to make it to Camp 2. My symptoms were getting worse, however, so I got straight into my sleeping bag after taking on more water. The next day was an acclimatisation day, where we rested for the morning before heading off towards Shipton's Camp, gaining the necessary height before turning around and heading back to camp. It was during this time that I began to vomit and also started suffering from diarrhoea, so when I returned I headed straight back into the tent with the view to start the summit attempt fresh the following day. I had now not eaten for over two days and could no longer hold anything down, only able to drink water.

The group all woke up eager to commence the summit push, but I had gone from bad to worse. The expedition leader spoke to me about turning back, but I was adamant that I was going to push on, so we agreed that I would stay at the back of the group whilst he stayed alongside. We headed out, but within 10 minutes my vomiting and diarrhoea had returned in spades – I was projecting vomit and diarrhoea simultaneously, unable to hold anything down. The leader allowed me to carry on for another 50 minutes before calling time, stating that I simply had to go back down. This was not good – and the last thing I wanted – but he was in charge and he could obviously tell I was in a bad way, knowing that I'd soon be battling altitude sickness as well. We had a brief debate before he called over one of the guides from our party.

We were now three days into the climb – a long way from civilisation and any form of rescue. I was told that we would walk back down the mountain until we reached the track, where at some point I'd be picked up by a Land Rover to be transferred to Nairobi Hospital. I had walked 17 miles up that same track three days earlier, realising that most parts were not accessible by any type of vehicle and that days of heavy rain had now turned it into a quagmire. This was a case of self-rescue – so although I felt so sick and weak, and although all I wanted to do was get into a sleeping bag, I turned around, faced downhill, and parted company with the expedition leader. I was truly gutted – again, failure entered my world, but I was not going to let this get into my mindset. Like Battle Camp, I had to focus on the here and now, and – besides – this was now down to personal survival. I needed to get off the mountain and lose height fast, whilst appreciating that I didn't have time or energy for toilet stops. I took the decision to stuff tissue into my boxer shorts, knowing I wouldn't be able to hold off the diarrhoea. As I headed downhill, I started to focus on drinking the bottle of Coke that would be waiting for me at my destination, whilst not knowing if the Land Rover was six, twelve, or twenty-four hours away from me.

It was tough. The guide was excellent, carrying my equipment and talking words of encouragement, but all I wanted to do was go to sleep. I had no energy, I couldn't hold any food down, and I was even throwing my medication back up. I remained focused on my objective, though – to get off the mountain fast – and counted down the miles. Finally, we made it to the track – the end was now in sight, although the track was no longer visible, looking more like a riverbed.

I took on more water and continued downwards. The vomiting and diarrhoea had not stopped, now turning into a watery liquid, and the smell was dreadful, but at that moment in time it didn't matter; I wasn't concerned, I just needed to meet up with the driver who would take me to hospital. After 10 hours of walking, I finally saw the Land Rover in the distance – the driver had managed to negotiate a few miles further up the muddy track. I was so happy – I was now on my last legs, with no fuel left in the tank. I was done.

It seemed that the three-point turn he had to manoeuvre first was the hardest part of his journey – it appeared to take him forever to complete. Somehow I managed to climb into the vehicle with the assistance from the guide to commence the journey back into Nairobi, stopping first at a village to purchase the bottle of Coke that had kept me going – I sipped it slowly, realising this was the first thing I had tasted other than water for over three days. I smelt terrible, so whilst on the stop I also changed my underwear and trousers, throwing the old ones away in the process.

When I finally arrived at Nairobi Hospital I was seen straight away, being taken away to give blood before being issued antibiotics and fluids. I was told to rest and report back in two days' time, which I did, to be told that I had contracted E. coli. I had lost a significant amount of weight and was reliably informed that the decision to turn back was the right thing to do, as – had I stayed on the mountain any longer – my body would have gone rapidly downhill, which could have led to shock and potentially a life threatening situation. Full respect to the expedition leader who made the right choice. I had failed to summit, but I had got back to camp and made a good recovery – on balance, a good outcome.

I met the guide again, who had been excellent in helping me off the mountain, and told him I was grateful for his assistance. I remembered him asking me about my Gore-Tex jacket and walking boots early on in the expedition, so to show my gratitude, I gave them to him – he was now the envy of all the Kenyan guides, walking around in his brand new clothing.

I remained in cadets for a further six months before deciding to leave. I had gained so much experience whilst at the same time passing on many life skills to young people, ultimately giving something back, and I'd also had the opportunity of taking some of these people throughout their entire cadet journey – entering the unit on day one as shy, unassuming individuals, and then developing into confident young people going on to gain qualifications and personal qualities that would make them stand out from their contemporaries.

A good example of this was when a shy girl entered the unit at the age of twelve, suffering with low self-esteem issues after being bullied at school. As a result, she initially struggled to engage in any form of activity that was put in front of her. Fast forward five years – she went on to become the senior cadet of the unit, responsible for organising evening parades and instructing lessons to junior cadets on a regular basis. The icing on the cake was when she was recognised as 'Best Cadet' on her Master Cadet Course – definitely job done!

In 2019, REBOOT was launched by the Police & Crime Commissioner (PCC) for Sussex. This was a Sussex Police-led programme, working with a range of partners to reduce the risk of young people becoming either the victim of or suspect of crime. As part of this early intervention programme, young people brought to the attention of the police are given the opportunity to join the Army Cadet Force.

The PPC stated, *"I want to give vulnerable young people in Sussex, who come to the attention of the police, a variety of opportunities to turn their lives around for the better"*. Clearly, the foundations laid down by Octavia Hill back in 1889 were still as relevant and effective more than 130 years later.

21

KIDS, SPORT & HOLIDAYS

I had grown up with discipline, respect, and sport as defined standards from an early age, with my parents' ensured discipline and respect taking precedence from as far back as I can remember. This was further endorsed by the middle school teacher who embossed his authority by defining the line in the sand – which we all learnt very quickly not to cross. My parents then encouraged me further by pushing me into sport, but it was my decision to take up martial arts that ensured discipline would remain pivotal in my life; studying under Shihan meant that these strict standards were going to be maintained. It was tough going; earning the right to wear the black belt was hard work, especially under Shihan. Years later, I learnt that Shihan was still highly regarded, cementing the fact that I'd been trained by the best.

Understanding the benefits I'd gained from these values in my own childhood, I made it my duty to pass these same values on to my children. During the early years my partner and I jointly ensured that discipline featured highly at home, but not on the scale I'd been exposed to. After all, it was obvious that these were very different times, the corporal punishment I'd endured throughout my school years having now been removed – teachers who once ruled by fear were no longer able to do so. Parents were also clashing with new agendas, and the power once held had somehow levelled out; the Victorian teachings I'd witnessed were long gone. The word 'No' had turned into a debate between adult and child. The hardest part was trying to maintain a consistent approach, as we'd often clash on certain issues. Despite this, we navigated our way through putting down essential markers, ensuring that acceptable standards became the benchmark.

I was also brought up to respect all adults and persons of authority, especially those in the uniformed services. Respect – like discipline – was drilled into me from an early age. Martial arts had endorsed my teachings, whilst being in the military taught me how respect was critical for the army to function effectively, with the armed forces adopting this standard over many years. Values passed on throughout their school years still remain with my children today – the values taught to me by my parents have been successfully passed on, although admittedly they are slightly more watered-down versions. Recognising the importance and benefits of sport, my secret weapon became pushing both boys into activities where they would be further exposed to these traits.

The first activity I was introduced to at school was gymnastics, which set out the foundations for my future sporting disciplines. Gymnastics is widely recognised as having broad benefits for building core strength and flexibility – all important transferable skills.

As I worked closely with the local gymnastics club, I was able to jump the long waiting list, allowing both my boys to commence with recreational gymnastics before progressing to the boys squad. This necessitated being trained in six disciplines, referred to as 6 Piece: floor, vault, bar, parallel bars, pommel, and rings. They both took an instant liking to it and were soon training 10 hours per week. This training was tough, with many hours spent perfecting their disciplines.

After two years they both took up football with local teams, meaning they had little time left for anything else – Andrew played in goal, with Luke opting for defence, playing for different teams in local leagues. Both activities started clashing and, after much debate, a decision was made: football was the winner. Gymnastics required more commitment, increasing to over 16 hours per week – time the boys (and I) just didn't have. Although they were disappointed to leave, the benefits they'd gained over those three years were significant, laying down exactly the same foundations gymnastics had gifted me with.

Andrew only managed two seasons of football before taking up BMXing as his main interest, and he went on to mountain biking and a great love for the outdoors. Luke went on to play football for over 10 years, remaining in the same team and achieving many great accolades. The team were encouraged from a young age to adopt a winning mentality, something that was slowly being lost at a grassroots level. This activity was great – it allowed routine to be harnessed, and a competitive sporting environment to be appreciated, where failure and success were experienced on a regular basis. By the time the team were teenagers they were playing in recognised top youth leagues, travelling around Sussex, Surrey, and London. Their most successful season came during 2013/14 where they were crowned league champions, league cup winners, Sussex County Cup champions, and were also awarded the Fair Play Award – a quadruple result, recognised as a first by any Sussex youth team.

Having two children who were fit and who played sport certainly influenced our holiday choices. We would head off on holiday to mainland Europe, for instance, where we would always embark on some form of adventurous training – walking, climbing, or water-based activities such as scuba diving.

Following my climb on Mont Blanc, I introduced the family to skiing with a trip to Chamonix. Everybody took to it straight away, valuing this activity first for the actual skiing and then for the mountain environment. Our favourite destination became Andorra and, in particular, the resort of Pas de la Casa, where we started travelling to for guaranteed snow and Pyrenees sunshine. During the first two trips to Pas, Jayne and the boys would spend the morning at ski school, giving me some time on my own before meeting back up early afternoon, at which point they would get to put their new skills to the test. They progressed well, with Andrew deciding to switch to snowboarding early on – a defining moment for him. The time spent in gymnastics proved pivotal as, within two years, both boys were riding black runs and taking on the jumps in the snow park.

We made skiing our annual family trip, always returning to Andorra; the town was great and the mountains even better, allowing all-day skiing across to other resorts within Andorra. We would always make the first run of the day – ensuring maximum time on the snow – with a quick rest stop for lunch to take on fuel before heading out again for the rest of the afternoon. It was during one of these days, high on a mountain, that we experienced a total whiteout. I had first experienced a whiteout whilst mountaineering in Wales, and that had been scary, but this time I would know how to react.

The weather had changed in minutes; we'd headed off early that morning in bright sunshine but the weather had worsened throughout the day with cloud quickly turning to snow, followed by high winds, and then – inevitably – the whiteout at the top of the mountain. Visibility was down to less than a metre, the piste was no longer visible, and we couldn't work out which way was up and which way was down. Fortunately, there were some other skiers high on the mountain as well, so I got us close together before we started following them, hoping they knew their way to safety. Within minutes the ski patrol arrived and took charge of the situation, taking us down the mountain and back to safety. This was real exposure in a wild environment, and while it was a tense situation as we made our way down the mountain, it was a good experience for everyone to learn: always respect your environment.

During the late nineties, I travelled back to Australia on my own three times over three consecutive years – I wanted to make a return ten years after I'd first visited Sydney. The third visit came when my brother and his partner planned a trip there in 2000, the year Sydney was hosting the Olympic Games. They were going to fly into Cairns from Alice Springs and then travel down the whole of the east coast. I wanted to do this route myself, as it had escaped me in 1988 when I only got as far up as Airlie Beach before turning around and heading south, back towards Sydney. The timing wasn't particularly good – Luke was only six months old at the time – but I really wanted to go, so after several heated discussions I booked my flights with the proviso that Mum would assist with looking after Luke. Fortunately, my mum did indeed come to the rescue, allowing me to head down to Cairns.

The trip turned out to be excellent. We backpacked down the whole east coast, staying in backpacker hostels, with a full-on inventory. The highlights of the trip included a three-day advanced PADI diving course on a liveaboard cruiser, and then visiting the Olympic Stadium in Sydney to watch the Australian qualifying games for the Olympics.

The PADI course allowed me to experience early morning and night diving in shark-infested waters on the Great Barrier Reef, which included tests consisting of a number of tasks you had to pass in order to qualify as an advanced diver. One test involved diving down to a depth of approximately 20 metres – in twos – to bring a heavy object back up to the surface, in a controlled manner and using the air from our oxygen tanks. We listened to the brief and were then told to discuss how we were going to approach this task.

My enthusiasm got the better of me, as I turned to my brother and said, "Don't worry; we'll just sort it out at the bottom." With that, I placed the regulator into my mouth and jumped into the sea, with my brother following close behind. Needless to say, when we got to the bottom, we just looked at each other. Shit. We hadn't discussed our strategy and were now unable to communicate. Despite this, however, we somehow managed to get through the task and we both went on to pass the course. Even to this day, my brother won't let me forget the words I said during that challenge.

More holidays followed to Florida, Dubai, and Tenerife. We all love Tenerife as it gives us some much-needed winter sun and is only a four-hour flight away. Due to this, Tenerife has become our go-to destination for both summer and winter holidays.

Once the boys were older, we were able to venture further afield on our own. India was at the top of Jayne's list, although the country never really appealed to me. After much debate, however, we decided to go for it. Jayne did the research and decided on visiting the Golden Triangle – this being the cities of Delhi, Agra, and Jaipur – and then adding a further five days in Goa.

We landed in Delhi – an enormous city covering 1,484 square kilometres – and headed out straight away, deciding to take a tuk tuk from our hotel lobby so that we could really appreciate the heavily congested streets. We didn't take the address of the hotel with us, so when – after an hour or so – we told the driver we should start to head back, all we got was a blank stare! We had no idea where we were or how far away we were from our hotel. The driver couldn't speak a word of English, so we had to drive around until we found someone who could speak at least a little bit of broken English, who then conveyed the name of our hotel to the driver. As Delhi is so heavily congested, with a population exceeding 18 million, and as it no doubt had lots of hotels with the same or similar name, this was a tall order – especially as we didn't even know what district we were in. Another hour passed before we managed to get back to our hotel – lesson learnt: always carry the business card of the hotel. The following day we took a guided tour of Delhi, looking at the city's amazing architecture, including visiting the resting place of Mahatma Gandhi.

We then travelled by train to Agra, the home of the Taj Mahal. As we approached this iconic building we couldn't help but be in total awe of what was standing in front of us. This building, which is constructed of white marble, was built by Mughal Emperor Shah Jahan in memory of his wife. It had been commissioned in 1632, and took about 16 years to construct. I think everyone should visit this building just for its sheer brilliance, especially considering it was constructed almost 400 years ago and was built to perfection in terms of symmetry, long before laser levels and specialist lifting equipment was readily available.

We then travelled to Jaipur, the capital of Rajasthan, where we spent the morning at the impressive Amber Fort – elephants would walk daily up to the top of the Fort. The city of Jaipur was painted pink over a century ago in honour of a visiting prince, and it has retained this colour ever since. Jaipur had originally been built by a notable astronomer, Maharaja Jai Singh, and we made sure to visit the Observatory too, which was amazing – I loved witnessing the connection to the moon, stars, and our solar system.

We left Jaipur to head to Mumbai before getting a connecting flight to Goa, where we stayed in a beach hut and spent a lot of time in beach bars and the many restaurants there. The people of Goa were truly humble, making us feel very welcome – so much so that we returned for a longer stay the following year.

By now Andrew had established himself as a snowboard instructor; from that first day on the snow back in Chamonix, and then switching to snowboarding in Andorra, he was now teaching individual and group lessons in British Columbia (BC), Canada. He had put his time to good use, gaining valuable experience and the necessary professional qualifications. He had come a long way, having found his true calling in life.

We visited him twice during his stay, giving us the chance to witness the splendour of this great country. We landed in Calgary and hired a jeep for the drive across the Rocky Mountains to his resort of Panorama, sitting high above the town of Invermere. En route, we stopped at the Calgary Olympic Park – home to the 1988 Winter Olympics, where Eddie the Eagle became the first English ski jumper to compete in both the 70 and 90 metre events since 1928.

He came last in both events, but his lack of success actually propelled him into the spotlight – nobody remembers who won the gold medal, but everyone remembers Eddie the Eagle! At the closing ceremony, the president of the Organising Committee noted the contribution made by Edwards, stating: "Some of you have soared like an eagle."

We skied together, with Andrew taking a few days off to show us the best runs and the high spa pools. During that trip we enjoyed the best of both worlds – skiing in the mountains during the day and then staying in the town at night, with access to all the local amenities. We also used the opportunity to visit Banff, Lake Louise, and Niagara Falls.

As I'd done years earlier, I found myself visiting Sydney again over three consecutive years. My friend Phil – who I'd met many years earlier at the Gatwick Hilton, en route to my first blind date – was now living in Sydney with his wife and had invited me over. I had such a good time in Sydney again that I went back twice more, rediscovering the city's beaches and bars. These days, Phil is living in Cambodia – time to start planning my next trip!

22

BIG FIVE ZERO

During the summer of 2012 the United Kingdom staged the Olympic Games. I had witnessed London winning the right to host the games seven years earlier at Trafalgar Square, and now it was finally happening.

London 2012 was recognised as a sporting triumph, with Team GB's performance being recorded as their greatest ever. They finished third in the medal table, winning 65 medals overall: 29 gold, 17 silver, and 19 bronze. Prime Minister David Cameron stated, *"It's lifted the whole country, brought people together, and it's been a fantastic performance. I'm very proud of what we've done."*

The London Olympics left a lasting legacy, not only with the facilities created in the Olympic Park but also by inspiring a whole generation to take up sport. I witnessed this locally, with sports participation across our facilities exceeding 1.4 million over the next year.

David Cameron had promised the country the opportunity to vote to either stay in or leave the European Union (EU) in a referendum, later referred to as the Brexit referendum. The vote took place on the 23rd June 2016.

In the end, the United Kingdom voted to leave the EU by 52% to 48% – only the slightest of margins, dividing the country in two. When final ballots were cast, early exit polls suggested the Remain campaign had won, but as votes were counted throughout the night and into the next morning, it became obvious that the Leave party – with Boris Johnson at the helm – were victorious. The UK was now poised to leave the EU in just under three years' time.

The Brexit vote was held close to my 50th birthday. At the time I was living with my brother, his wife, and their children as I had hit the wall, going through a change of my own: the midlife crisis. I had spent so much time with my sons, but now they'd moved on; they were no longer reliant on me and were getting on with their own lives. Most of my evenings and weekends had been taken up with driving to various activities, but those days were over. Now I found myself waking up at weekends with very little to do; the boys were busy, and I was feeling lost.

On a positive note, it was job done – the boys had become independent, and were starting to carve out their own plans. On balance, this was positive, though the negative was that the timing wasn't particularly good, corresponding with a significant birthday. The thought of turning 50 was daunting enough; it was a significant milestone, and now I was left trying to find purpose again.

I had experienced this before when I'd first left the Army and was transitioning back into civilian life, which resulted in me travelling to Australia to be with a woman I barely knew. I was going through a similar chapter in my life now, with major change being the common link. The only way I could deal with this was to move out of the family home and in with my brother, with the intention of 'sorting my shit out'. The last time I'd heard that phrase was back in 1989 from my dad – years later, I was now the catalyst.

My oldest son likened my situation to wanting to drive off into the sunset on a Harley-Davidson motorbike with a younger woman in tow. I was in real turmoil, not knowing which way to turn, not knowing whether to stay or go. I was just so confused, and I actually managed to convince myself that I needed to go out and meet another woman – a better option, maybe. I actually researched the benefits of having an affair, identifying all the pros and cons. I thought a lot about the prospect of being with another woman, and all the benefits that would bring. This process went on for quite some time until I finally worked out that the positive reasons for staying far outweighed the Harley-Davidson scenario.

I had climbed Mont Blanc when I was forty and now I wanted to add another big mountain to my name. The most obvious and iconic for any mountaineer to attempt was, of course, Mount Everest.

Mount Everest – known locally as Sagarmatha (Nepalese for 'goddess of the sky') – is the world's highest mountain, with an elevation of 8,848m (29,031 ft.). The first official ascent was made in 1953 by Sherpa Tenzing Norgay and Edmund Hillary, the same year Queen Elizabeth II acceded the throne. Whilst researching the climb, however, it became apparent to me that it was going to be an unlikely thing for me to accomplish, as the prerequisite was two months away from work and a budget amounting to thousands of pounds, rendering it impossible. Therefore, I opted instead to trek to Everest Base Camp with my eldest son, Andrew.

The two of us flew to Kathmandu. The capital of Nepal, it is surrounded by the Himalayas and stands at 1,400m, allowing precious little time to acclimatise. It took over an hour for us to get through customs, and when we finally exited into the car park we were met by groups of people wanting to carry our equipment to the waiting taxis. I had become agitated because of the delay, so when I was approached by two men I allowed them to carry our bags, without thinking too much about it. After placing our bags into the boot of a car, they held out their hands for payment. I took some money out of my pocket, and with that, $40 was snatched. I asked the taxi driver if these were our guides, to which he replied, *"No, they are bad people."* So, I ran over to retrieve my money, though I only managed to recover $20. Not a good start, but a wake-up call to stay alert.

After two days spent visiting local sites of interest, we packed up our expedition equipment for the transfer from Kathmandu airport to Lukla. Lukla is regarded as one of the most dangerous runways in the world due to its close proximity to the mountains and the often inclement weather. We waited all morning for the cloud to break at Lukla before finally boarding the small twin prop aircraft for the short transfer.

When we landed at Lukla – which stands at 2,840m, almost twice the height of Ben Nevis in Scotland – we were introduced to our climbing team, all men local to Nepal. We carried out our final equipment checks and then headed out into the Khumbu Valley. After four hours we arrived at the first tea house in Phakding – tea houses provide accommodation and food stops during the trek. After being allocated our rooms, we tried out the local cuisine – in this case, garlic soup followed by *Momos* (dumplings) served with rice – before settling down for the evening, giving us time to socialise with the other group members. We were a group of twelve in total, all of us international travellers with limited mountaineering experience. It soon became obvious that I was the eldest, my son the youngest. The conversation focused on altitude sickness and worries of not making it to Base Camp, leading to some of the group buying specialist medication to try to help against this threat. I remember telling my son that this was new territory for everyone; having witnessed the effects of altitude before, I was convinced some would struggle.

The next day we woke early, had breakfast, checked our equipment, then headed out back into the Khumbu Valley towards the prosperous trading town of Namche Bazaar. This was going to become the standard routine – up early, walk all day with small rest stops, and have a light lunch before arriving at the next tea house either early or late afternoon, at which point we would rest up.

The steep ascent started after crossing the iconic foot bridges in high ravines with fast-flowing rivers below. The final part of the climb was a steep two-hour ascent up Namche Hill to reach Namche Bazaar, the capital of the Khumbu region, standing at over 3,400m. We spent two days in Namche acclimatising, which gave us time to explore this bustling capital.

Namche Hill was the location of the first incident. One of the group – a Columbian man judged to be the fittest member – suddenly lost all sense of direction before appearing totally confused. He went from acting completely normal to having a total meltdown in a matter of minutes. The leader tried to calm him down, but he was having none of it; he walked off at pace into the distance, stating that he needed to get to the next rest stop quickly. The leader didn't show any concern – saying we'd catch up to him in due course – and as it turned out, he was right; as we entered Namche, we found the man sitting under a tree, his head between his legs. He was then escorted to the tea house, where he was given a large meal before being sent to bed. He woke the following morning with no recollection of his actions the previous day. The mountains had claimed their first victim – a wake-up call for the remainder of the group, all of whom were left wondering who was going to be next.

Namche was full of street markets and tea houses catering for trekkers from all over the world. There were also bakeries and restaurants which, once you were sitting inside, could easily be mistaken for English eateries, as they were modern and served fantastic food. It really is a testament to the supply chain of Nepalese porters who carry hordes of essential supplies up the mountain paths daily from Lukla.

Sited high above the village, I got my first view of Mount Everest – a truly emotional experience signalling that we were now within reach of this legendary mountain.

Acclimatisation done, we left Namche to walk the well-worn trail, following the contours around the valley high above the Dudh Kosi en route to Debouche. We took on the steep climb to

Thyangboche, stopping off on the way to visit the famous monastery. This steep climb claimed another victim: a bodybuilder whose body was not made for this type of environment. He was struggling with the altitude and falling ever further behind. Fortunately, help was on hand, and he was assisted slowly up to the next location. We pushed on to reach the village of Debouche – standing at 3,700m – and then we rested up for the night.

The next day was going to be significant, as we were now heading into serious altitude territory with our aim of reaching Dingboche, standing at 4,410m. The leader reminded the group of the necessity to keep a slow pace, to break the climb down into small chunks, and to only focus on the next objective, which for us was Dingboche. This reminded me again of the same lessons I'd learnt on Mont Blanc. The guide also reminded us that a helicopter was only a phone call away, should anyone wish to abandon the climb. Definitely not an option!

After breakfast we carried out the obligatory kit check before trekking through rhododendrons to Pangboche, where we got to witness Ama Dablam – which translates as 'Mother's Necklace' – up close. Standing at 6,812m, it truly is an iconic mountain. The long ridges of the mountain on either side look like the arms of a mother (Ama) protecting her child, hence the name. We continued contouring up through the Imja valley until we reached the farming village of Dingboche, signalling the second acclimatisation rest stop of the trek. This was timely as, by now, three members of the group had started to suffer from headaches and tingling sensations in their hands. It had also started to snow, so it was a good time for everyone to rest, to take stock, and to start making preparations for the next stage. It soon became apparent that those suffering with tingling sensations had taken medication to starve off the altitude sickness and were seemingly having a bad reaction to it. Needless to say, they stopped taking it straight away. By now the weather had closed in, and it stayed that way for the remainder of our time spent at Dingboche – before clearing in readiness for the trek towards Lobuje.

The weather had changed again, now turning into brilliant sunshine with a gentle breeze as we headed up the steep climb beside the glacial moraine towards Lobuje. This was my bad day – I felt nauseous, had totally lost my appetite, and was left feeling weak. Then we reached another rest stop, allowing me time to recover before the final push. I was confused. After all, I had done well so far – my son and I had been at the front for the whole trek, and I'd felt good. Still feeling bad, I went to sleep at 4,940m knowing that over the next 24 hours I would be standing at Base Camp in full view of Mount Everest.

I awoke feeling much better and, after an early breakfast, we headed out towards Gorak Shep, located at 5,200m. We were now really high, walking above 5,000m, feeling the true impact of altitude, which for me meant a headache and shortness of breath. When we arrived at Gorak Shep, the site of Sir Edmund Hillary's 1953 expedition's base camp, we left our kit before taking on food and water. We all got called together, at which point our guides checked that we were all feeling well enough to continue on to Base Camp, a 90-minute walk at 5,364m.

Finally, we arrived at Everest Base Camp, where I got to see the array of yellow expedition tents with rows and rows of prayer flags. This was where the expedition teams for the 2016 climbing season were based, in a cold, stark place situated in front of the famous Khumbu Icefall at the foot of the Western Cwm on the slopes of Mount Everest.

The icefall is often considered by many climbers to be the most dangerous area on the South Col route up to the summit. When we arrived, there seemed to be a lot of activity; helicopters landing with medical teams on board signalled that something was happening higher up the mountain.

In April 2015, a powerful earthquake had struck Nepal, killing 9,000 people and injuring over 22,000 more. The earthquake had also triggered an avalanche on Mount Everest, killing 19 people at

Base Camp and effectively ending all attempts to reach the peak that year. A year earlier, a massive ice fall on a glacier on the main climbing route killed 16 people, rendering the route impassable for the whole season. This year there were 34 teams booked to attempt the summit, and all were desperate to make it to the roof of the world – whenever the weather window presented itself.

On 11th May, a team of nine Sherpas made the climb from Base Camp to the summit, fixing ropes along the way for other climbers to utilise. The day after, UK climber Kenton Cool achieved his 12th summit. I had arrived at Base Camp to be told that there were 20 separate climbing teams attempting to summit.

We headed back towards Gorak Shep, where we checked in to the tea house for our last night. There were no amenities on site; it was very basic accommodation. Most of the team were not feeling well, and all were suffering with headaches – expected symptoms at above 5,000m. It was the worst night's sleep of the trek. We awoke early, then had breakfast before heading back down the mountain for the 65km trek back to Lukla.

During the weekend we'd spent at Gorak Shep and Base Camp, there were several reported deaths on the mountain. A Dutch climber and Australian woman were reported to have died suffering from altitude sickness. Four Indian climbers got lost high on the mountain – three were later found dead, with the one survivor being evacuated to Kathmandu. Other climbers were also reported to have died on the mountain.

The Indian climbers were part of the South Korean-led expedition team who were staying at our hotel, and we watched as the media interviewed the surviving team member and expedition leader. I had loved witnessing the beauty of Nepal and the Himalayas, but watching the interview reminded me of the dangers of trying to summit Everest.

23

STAY AT HOME

The first time I heard about COVID-19 was early January 2020, when media reports cited a mystery virus had appeared in China, the source: the city of Wuhan. Initial reports stated that the virus was likely to flare up for a short while before disappearing altogether.

My first personal connection with the virus was during a holiday to Tenerife that February. I was sitting in the apartment when a breaking news story came on the TV, stating that an individual travelling from an 'at risk' region in Italy had presented himself to a hospital in Tenerife with symptoms of an acute respiratory infection. After being tested, he was confirmed as having COVID-19. This led to the hotel and all its guests being placed in quarantine – an action that made global headlines. That's right: COVID-19 had made its way onto this isolated island and was now less than five miles from where I was staying, making me realise the virus was no longer contained in China.

By early March the virus had taken hold throughout Italy, with hospitals now full of COVID patients – the country was facing a major crisis. Based on the news coming out of Italy, Government Scientific Advisors started calling for an immediate UK lockdown in order to start making preparations for the potential fallout. At this point, mass gatherings were still happening in the UK, including Atlético Madrid playing in the Champions League against Liverpool, with many away fans travelling from Madrid – recognised at the time as the centre of Spain's COVID outbreak.

As it still felt, however, like the virus was still a long way off, we decided to visit Andrew, who was working in Austria. So, we flew to Munich and caught the train down to Austria, arriving in the town of Ehrwald. We arrived on the Friday and everything appeared normal, although it soon became clear that COVID was the main topic of conversation. We skied all day Saturday, during which everything remained normal – all bars and restaurants were open and the resort was full. When we turned up on Sunday morning to meet up with Andrew at ski school, however, we found out there was a rumour that Austria was considering closing down its borders. Despite these warnings, we carried on.

As the day went on the resort started to empty out, and by mid-afternoon the place was almost bare. We continued to ski, but then the bars and restaurants all started closing down, which was really odd and didn't feel right at all. We continued doing what we were doing until the whole resort became totally empty – we were the last people on the snow, and it just felt so strange and eerie. After skiing the last run of the day we went to the only bar still open, finishing up with a cold beer.

After our drink we caught the bus back to the hotel, where we were met by the owner; he came running over, looking panicked, and told us, "You have to pack and leave the country straight away as all public transport is being closed down and the borders are closing tonight!" Shit. This had turned serious – we were literally being told to pack up and go. By this point Andrew had been in Austria for three months, and now he had to leave without any warning. Fortunately, the owner offered to drive us to the border town of Garmisch-Partenkirchen.

Within three hours we had walked off the snow, packed, and were now en route to Germany before the borders closed that night. After a tense drive through Austria, having had to negotiate a number of checkpoints, we finally arrived in Garmisch, being dropped off at the train station in time to meet the connecting train to Munich Airport.

The news coming out of Germany was that they were also preparing to close their borders, so when we arrived we decided to change our flights to early morning in an attempt to beat any exodus. Due to the rapidly changing situation we decided to camp down in the terminal for the night – we managed to stay in McDonalds for a couple of hours before being asked to leave, so it was going to be a night on the wooden benches in the terminal. A new experience for the boys!

I arrived back home on the Monday, at which point the landscape was clearly changing: major sport was being cancelled and attendances at the sport centres were declining daily, to the point where the operator was trying to force a closure. During this week, medical experts came up with several scientific models based on the current rate of infection, identifying that COVID could lead to between 250,000 and 500,000 deaths – clearly, drastic action was now required.

By the Friday, we were in discussions with the Head of Finance with a view to close the centres that day at midnight. Then, at 5.00 p.m. that night, the Prime Minister, Boris Johnson, made a statement instructing the nation to work from home and to only travel if it was essential. He also stated that pubs, clubs, theatres, and sport centres were to close that night – Boris Johnson had made the tough decision for us! The scientific modelling numbers had been the game changer; another week and the National Health Service (NHS) would soon be at saturation point.

So, the government had made the call to close all the venues I had responsibility for. This was completely new territory for the country, and the first time anything like this had occurred since the Second World War. I joined the senior management team call later that evening to take stock of the situation and to agree on the response – the sport centre had been seconded as an emergency food distribution and medical supply station for Sussex. This would entail taking large deliveries of food coming in from superstores that would then be split up into individual food parcels, before being sent out to vulnerable residents. Medical supplies were sourced from local pharmacies and delivered direct.

On the 23rd March, Boris Johnson appeared on television again with those now famous words – "You Must Stay at Home" – as the country entered full lockdown. There were a reported 186 deaths on the day lockdown was announced; just two weeks later, the death toll had exceeded 1,000. Within a very short time the country had completely changed. There were deserted streets and roads, with most shops and amenities now being closed, as all workers had been instructed to work from home if they could.

Even at this point, it still felt like COVID was somebody else's problem and unlikely to impact us; this was certainly the case with a lot of young people, who were still going about their daily business as normal. A single event, however, was about to bring a sweeping mind shift across the nation.

I was sitting at home when a breaking news story splashed across the television screen: '*Boris Johnson has been admitted to Hospital*'. This was massive news – the person at the helm of the country tasked with fighting this disease was now a casualty himself. It then went from bad to very bad – the next news story stated that he had been moved into intensive care, with his condition deteriorating overnight. This was really worrying; if the disease could find its way into the Prime Minister's residence, surely we were all vulnerable. This was a real wake-up call for the entire country, causing attitudes to change almost overnight. Nobody wanted any harm to come to Boris Johnson – he was in charge and he still had the fight to win. Fortunately, he made a good recovery, which was followed by some time off at his country retreat before returning to work – phew, a close call!

By the summer some of the European countries were starting to reopen their borders, so in July we took the opportunity to go back out to Tenerife for a few days. This coincided with the UK lockdown ending and the opening up of sport centres, gyms, and shops. We flew out on the Friday afternoon, as planned, and headed straight out, enjoying our newly restored freedom. We were sitting in a local bar on the Saturday evening when a new breaking news story appeared – the Canary Islands were deemed to be at risk by the UK government due to mainland Spain reporting high infection rates. They were then put on the list of countries deemed as 'essential travel only', requiring all returning holiday makers to self-isolate (to not leave home) for 14 days. We thought we'd been returning to some normality, but now we were plunged straight back into staying at home for a further two weeks.

Over the next three months we did return to some form of normality – with restrictions being lifted further and further – and the sport centre was making a good recovery, with numbers increasing week on week. We felt we were just starting to turn the corner in terms of getting back to 'normal' when further restrictions were imposed again, eventually leading to the second full lockdown – this time only lasting a month.

As we left the second lockdown, Christmas was nearly upon us, albeit with everyone recognising it would be a very different type of celebration this year. Christmas is a time for joy and hope – and that at least was the same this year, with news that the long-awaited vaccine was starting to be rolled out across the UK.

24

DOES HE FIGHT IT?

The birthday card I received from my son on my 53rd birthday summed up exactly how I was feeling at the time: it featured a bold caption declaring *'Does he fight it or let himself go?'* After battling through my midlife crisis, sorting out the indifferences in my life, I was now ready to commence the next battle. The previous card I received had depicted a photograph revealing my stomach with a question mark. The new card included three self-portraits; first, a photograph of me holding my shirt high above my waist, in the moment, then two bodies with a photograph of my head superimposed over the top. The first, a typical Joe Wicks (the UK's Body Coach) body shape, and then an obese body shape. They were standing side by side, telling me I had a tough choice to make. *Do I fight it or let myself go?*

Exercise has always been part of my DNA, and I've always recognised the importance of maintaining good health. The downside now was that I was no longer 21; even if my head thought I was, my body wasn't going to let me get away with it. The effects of the high impact sports I'd previously undertaken had now disappeared, with martial arts and competitive running being but distant memories, now having been replaced with low impact activities. Fitness had been replaced with maintenance. Exercise was key to staying in shape, but healthy eating was just as important, and I'd now recognised that my metabolic rate had slowed down. The final part was my mindset, which was hard to keep in check especially when there was so much temptation on offer. The birthday card, therefore, was a stark reminder warning me that it was going to take a disciplined approach to stay in shape. With this in mind, I took the time to look back and reflect on my previous experiences.

I was born 18 days before England won the FIFA World Cup in 1966 – which is still cited as the nation's greatest sporting triumph – and almost three years to the day when mankind would celebrate one of its greatest achievements: Apollo 11 successfully landing the Eagle Lunar Module on the moon, and astronaut Neil Armstrong stepping onto the moon's surface.

My parents' decision to move down from London in search of a better life was decisive, ensuring I had a childhood full of opportunity. The new towns were ideal for all those men and women wanting to leave London behind, and the environment was vital for our wellbeing. At the time the new town was still being planned, with new neighbourhoods still under construction, so the move to a brand new house in a cul-de-sac ensured we had a rich childhood. The area was full of green open spaces, guaranteeing I'd spend many hours outside, setting me up for future longings. The town was full of families searching for a better life; our parents had grown up throughout the Second World War, with many only experiencing life outside London as evacuees. There was a common thread running throughout the town – our parents had lived through hard times but now they were determined to gift their children a better life, and there was no better place to do so than my town.

Having positive role models gave me the best start in life by giving me the confidence to go out and explore the world. The new teacher brought a new dimension to middle school, with me quickly having to learn the consequences of crossing him. These were the days of corporal punishment, allowing teachers to rule the classroom by fear. Back then, you couldn't even tell your parents if you fell victim to punishment, as you knew they would side with the teacher.

One story regarding my dad's school days that he always reminiscenced about concerned his immaculately dressed teacher who ruled the classroom like a Sergeant Major, demanding respect and not taking any shit (my dad's words) from anyone. This was post-war Brixton, and times were tough. One day, during a normal lesson, the school 'hard man' was being rowdy and disruptive. Despite being warned several times to stop, he ignored the teacher and carried on regardless, being even more disruptive and stating he would 'knock the teacher out'. The teacher responded by telling him that if it was a boxing match he wanted, then a boxing match he would get. Within minutes the teacher and boy were standing toe-to-toe, trading blows. This went on for about five minutes, before the teacher called a halt to the proceedings. Both bloodied and bruised, they shook hands, and the boy sat down without saying a word to anyone. Needless to say, he was never disruptive again. I love this story for two reasons: the enthusiasm with which my dad tells it and the fact that this type of behaviour was acceptable back then. It certainly sorted out the immediate problem whilst demanding a new level of respect for the teacher.

Despite discipline being integral at home during my early years, I was a wayward child – especially at school – with most of my discretions being labelled 'mischievous'. As I was disciplined, however, I never had a self-destruct button, always knowing when to stop... or so I'd like to think! I wasn't at all academic, but would excel in most sports, so that's where my unspent energy would get channelled. Two important factors then came together for me: deciding to participate in martial arts and then the transition to secondary school.

My first involvement in sport came at school, with gymnastics and running, both aiding my transition into martial arts. At first I practised Judo, learning the key requirements: strength, flexibility, and balance, the same skills I'd learnt at gymnastics. The first thing I remember being taught (after the bow) was the 'forward roll break fall', which I would spend hours practising until I was perfect. This necessitated bringing both hands and the right foot forward simultaneously, before pushing strongly from both feet and tucking the right arm inward as I entered the roll. I then struck the mat with my hand as my feet made contact with the floor. This practice was followed by learning the back, forward, and side break fall techniques, employed solely to prevent injury and to minimise pain when thrown by any opponent. Judo taught me the importance of physical and mental discipline through the practice of attack and defence.

I left Judo for Karate after hearing about this mythical instructor who had trained in the Far East. Once I commenced training, it became clear that the style was deep-rooted in a philosophy of self-improvement and discipline. Training was tough and Shihan was formidable, with punishments being handed out for not meeting his standard.

Attending secondary school brought considerable change, as I'd now joined the top league and higher standards would become the norm, with a greater focus on learning now required. It was important not to bring any unwanted attention to yourself, as the first few weeks involved establishing territory with plenty of testosterone on display and fights aplenty. Being fit brought respect, and finishing in the top three of the mob run ensured I was never a target for bullies. I didn't mention martial arts at school as I knew this would throw down the gauntlet within certain quarters. I lived through the eighties' music scene, still cited by many as the greatest music decade ever, with dance music, new wave, rock, electro, and multi-million pound videos being shown on MTV all the time. Music artists like Madonna, Prince, The Police, and Duran Duran were plastered all over the t-shirts worn at school, becoming the unofficial school uniform.

My final school year was really busy. I was studying for my final exams knowing I had to attain good grades in order to progress through the army selection process. I was training every evening for my black belt grading, as well as running long distances in readiness for basic training. It was during this time that I got to stare failure in the face, with real consequences. During 1982 the

Army had reduced the number of recruit vacancies due to defence cuts, and I hadn't made the new standard. I was completely devastated as I had no desire to do anything else – it was the military or nothing – so I had to work on a plan B, and quickly. I took on extra maths lessons to improve my test results and then went up to Scotland on a two-week adventurous training course, gaining an excellent report. This corresponded with my final exams, in which I received the grades required to satisfy army selection. This was then followed by success at the grading and, after resitting the exam, I was offered a vacancy in the Royal Corps of Transport as a Junior Leader, commencing in January 1983.

Leaving home at 16 is tough on anybody, but to leave and immediately enter a brand new world of reward and punishment was on a completely different level. The screaming and shouting started as soon as I arrived, meaning I had to learn quickly and do exactly what was being asked of me. Within two hours we were changed and running, being given a guided tour of the camp, up close and personal. Clearly, my training programme was working to good effect; I felt strong and was able to keep up with the troop sergeant.

I quickly adopted the same approach I'd taken throughout secondary school – trying to blend in by becoming the grey man deemed critical for survival throughout the first term. The environment was very similar too, with plenty of testosterone on display and fights aplenty. The reward and punishment culture, with group reprimands, featured heavily throughout all three terms. It only took one person not meeting the standard for the whole troop to be punished, therefore it was vital not to fall short; this would always result in any disputes being resolved by fighting. The law of the jungle was quickly established, with only two options: stand up or fall victim.

My first posting was in West Germany, serving in the British Army of the Rhine (BAOR), the first line of defence against the Soviet

Union. I had spent school assemblies glued to government information videos warning of the threat from nuclear attack, and learning what actions to take when an attack was known to be imminent. Within a few years I was on the front line, playing out the Cold War for real – a game of strategy between East and West. The military hardware on display was immense; there were rows and rows all lined up ready for mobilisation at short notice, with over 53,000 highly trained military personnel at the ready.

Back-to-back tours followed, first down to the South Atlantic and then a six-month tour of Belize, before returning back to the Falkland Islands. These were busy tours in great locations, affording me brand new experiences working with the Navy and Royal Airforce (RAF). Working as part of the Field Surgical Team (FST) in Belize was a major highlight, especially participating in the important 'Hearts and Minds' role for the British Army. Belize was hard going, with tough living conditions; the jungle was recognised as the harshest of all military training environments, with the heat and humidity, the dense vegetation, and small bothersome insects aplenty.

I spent my final year in England realising my ambition of becoming a Physical Training Instructor (PTI). My time in Germany and my overseas tours had previously hampered any chances of promotion or of attending any training courses, and the United Kingdom opened up new opportunities for me. I took to the PTI course right away, excelling in all disciplines and receiving a recommendation to return on the advanced course. The icing on the cake was being a member of the winning section.

I had only known two things up until now: exercise and the military. The Army had given me a civilian sporting qualification, so the natural progression was into a career in sport and leisure. After a few months I got my dream job at the local sport centre, somewhere I'd spent a great deal of time during my childhood. Starting as a lifeguard, it wasn't long before I'd progressed into management roles whilst also maintaining my role as a fitness instructor. I remained at the sport centre until an opportunity arose at a community leisure centre, where I got to refocus my efforts, targeting wayward children in a hearts and minds campaign – to good effect. The success of these projects and a change in government legislation led to a new role, managing the portfolio of leisure facilities across the town. This was a great move as it led to project managing the construction of a brand new sport centre. I remained as part of a small team, setting up management and operational arrangements for the town's leisure facilities.

Both of my boys were born during the nineties. I felt like it was my duty to pass on the same skills taught to me by my parents, ensuring that discipline and respect took centre stage whilst also encouraging them to go into sport in the same way my parents did with me.

I remained busy, continuing to push and challenge myself as I approached forty, and choosing to climb Mont Blanc knowing it would be tough. Exercise remained pivotal. I got myself back into uniform and continued to push the envelope at work. Time was hurtling by – holidays, overseas military expeditions, Brexit, midlife crisis… and then the big Five Zero and beyond.

Now, as I enter the next chapter of my life, I continue to remain positive, disciplined and fully prepared to face any challenges that may lie ahead. I'm ready to fight it – I found FAME!

Epilogue

Make Your Bed

The first lesson taught on day one of basic training is how to make your bed – a thirty minute example of perfection. During this presentation you're taught how to present a 'Bed Box'. This is a symmetrical staging of sheets, blankets and pillows in a square 'box' shape, which is then centred under the headboard on a tightly pulled bed cover, finished off with razor-sharp hospital corners. This was critical; it was a key factor for any room inspection with guaranteed punishment for not meeting the standard. There was good reason why this was the first lesson.

Making your bed gets you into the right mindset for the day ahead. It is essentially the first task of the day and, if done well, it will give you a small sense of pride. Do this well and it will encourage you to do another task well, and then another well, and so on. If you do the little tasks right, it will encourage you to go on and complete the more important tasks to a good standard.

Embrace Failure

Failure is often considered a negative, but this is untrue. My own personal first experience of failure – with consequence – was rejection from the Army. I was devastated, but it forced me to quickly refocus on achieving the outcome required to gain entry to Junior Leaders.

Failure goes hand in hand with success. If you fail, try again; use the failure to improve the next time. Learn from your failure.

Ambition

I set my ambition early; I wanted to earn the right to wear a black belt in Karate, as I was in awe of all the instructors wearing this prized procession. Watching the SAS storm the Embassy, and the Falklands War, certified my desire to join the Army.

Be ambitious, and set goals – they give you direction. Treat them as stepping stones from where you are today to your hopes for the future. The direction of travel, planning, and working towards your goals are just as important as actually achieving them.

Tune into your Mindset

My mindset was shaped by my parents, my middle school teacher, and then the martial arts instructors, all of them setting me up for military basic training. We were informed on day one that we would become Champion Troop – there was no question about it.

Key decisions and outcomes are driven by mindset, with a good mindset making it possible for you to achieve positive results. Shift your mindset; viewing things differently will open up new opportunities.

Make Exercise Part of Your DNA

I started sport at school with gymnastics before progressing to martial arts. The earlier you start physical activity, the faster the payback.

Exercise makes you feel happier, helps with weight loss, reduces risk of serious illness, increases energy levels, and improves attitude. It's never too late to start, regardless of age, so give it a go.

Take Small Steps

Focus on the here and now – this is critical for reaching any summit. If you focus only on the summit, chances are you won't make it.

Focus on the immediate objective and then, once achieved, move onto the next one. Taking small steps increases the chances of meeting objectives, as well as ensuring you won't become too overwhelmed by what lies ahead.

Play the Long Game

Had I waited for the advanced PTI course, it could have led to a career in the Army School of Physical Training.

Be patient and be prepared for any knock-backs along the way. Too many people want things right now. As the saying goes, good things come to those who wait.

Ignore Doubters

When presenting the concept for the new sport centre, it was perceived by some as being too ambitious. These doubters were ignored, allowing the successful delivery of the project. It is still recognised as a top sporting venue today.

Most doubters sit in the 'glass half empty' category, offering a pessimistic view. Try not to surround yourself with too many people whose glasses are half empty.

Giving Back

I found satisfaction in watching changing attitudes from latchkey kids, which inspired me to join the Army Cadet Force.

Doing things for others – giving, and ultimately helping others – can be both powerful and rewarding. Pass on your skills and experience, allowing others to benefit from your knowledge.

Learning

Being curious about the karate instructor led to me getting absorbed in a new hobby and passion.

Learning is a rich source of enjoyment and happiness. Being curious, creative, and open to trying new things will help keep your brain in shape, will help you find fulfilment, and will allow you to get more out of life.

About the Author

Aged just 16, Paul Baker joined the British Army. He had a fulfilling career that led him all over the world – to places like Belize and the Falkland Islands – before he left to find his true vocation. He has over 30 years' experience working in the leisure industry – starting in the fitness sector and then moving into managing and designing sporting facilities.

Paul's martial arts background and army training taught him the importance of discipline and resilience, qualities he continues to use in all other areas of his life. Underlining everything he does is his knowledge of how mindset can set you up for success, how failure is a learning experience, and why exercise is so important for both body and mind.

Covid-19 was a real game changer; destroying lives, devastating economies, and exposing vulnerabilities, it was tough on everyone. March 2020, therefore, became the catalyst for Paul putting pen to paper and writing his memoir – an ambition years in the planning.

Paul now lives in Sussex with his partner and two children. He spends his leisure time walking and cycling, and – when time permits – he also enjoys mountaineering and international travel.

Write a Review

Thank you for reading my memoir. I hope you found it useful and enjoyed the story. If you did enjoy the story please leave a review where you purchased the book.

CPSIA information can be obtained
at www.ICGtesting.com
Printed in the USA
LVHW011626261021
701609LV00019B/519

9 781839 756634